D0997067

AND SO TO BED

AND SO TO BED

by Joanna Copestick

PAVILION

First published in Great Britain in 2000 by
PAVILION BOOKS LIMITED
London House, Great Eastern Wharf
Parkgate Road, London SW11 4NQ
www.pavilionbooks.co.uk

Text © Joanna Copestick 2000
Design and layout © Pavilion Books Ltd 2000.

The moral right of the author and illustrator
has been asserted

Designed by Jane Forster

And So To Bed products in the prelims: the Byron bed
(p2), various beds (pp4–5) and the Brodsworth (p7).

All rights reserved. No part of this publication
may be reproduced, stored in a retrieval system, or
transmitted, in any form or by any means, electronic,
mechanical, photocopying, recording or otherwise,
without the prior permission of the copyright holder.

A CIP catalogue record for this book is available
from the British Library.

ISBN 1 86205 391 X

Colour reproduction by Anglia Graphics, England.
Printed and bound in Singapore by Kyodo.

10 9 8 7 6 5 4 3 2 1

This book can be ordered direct from the publisher.
Please contact the Marketing Department. But try your
bookshop first.

AND SO TO BED —LONDON— is a registered trademark. The
company can be contacted as follows: by telephone on
01372 460660, by fax on 01372 460666 and
by email at enquiries@andsotobed.co.uk

contents

foreword

As one of the leading bed retailers, it is amusing that my story actually began with the purchase of a bed in the late sixties. The antique brass bedstead that I bought was too small for the mattress I wanted to use and so I decided to sell it on by putting an advertisement in a newspaper. The huge response was a great surprise. It was at this point that I realised there was actually a demand for good antique brass bedsteads, something which until that point I thought was just my personal taste. I started hunting around antiques shops at weekends for suitable bedsteads to renovate and sell.

Things took off and the first shop was opened in 1971. In those days we only sold antique beds. It wasn't long, however, before demand outstripped the supply and we began to manufacture reproductions. We now have a vast range of designs in wood, iron, brass and leather.

The bedroom is, I believe, the most personal room in a house, a place where you can indulge your own tastes and create a private sanctuary. The bed, of course, is the main element and will dictate the style of the room. My own tastes are rather traditional and while those styles continue to be popular, I also like to keep ahead of trends and am always striving to produce new designs to give people a broad spectrum from which to choose, whether a simple Japanese style or an elaborate four-poster.

Choosing a bed is an important decision and can affect both your sleeping and waking hours. Our beds are made to last, so your choice should be something that you know you can live with and a style that will stand the test of time. We always try to help people make an informed decision, taking into account how the bedroom is used, and the design statement they wish to make. The mattress is an equally important decision because this will be a significant health factor for many years.

The bed contributes to the overall atmosphere of the bedroom, but there are many other elements to consider. Over the years we have often been asked to recreate a whole 'And So To Bed' look and so have introduced complementary lines, including furniture, bedlinen and accessories. Each element plays a part in the ultimate goal of a good night's sleep.

The pages that follow are filled with styles and ideas, and I hope this book will be an inspiration, encouraging readers to be creative in their choice of bedsteads and accessories, resulting in a space within which they can relax and find peace and comfort.

Keith Barnett

introduction

a personal space

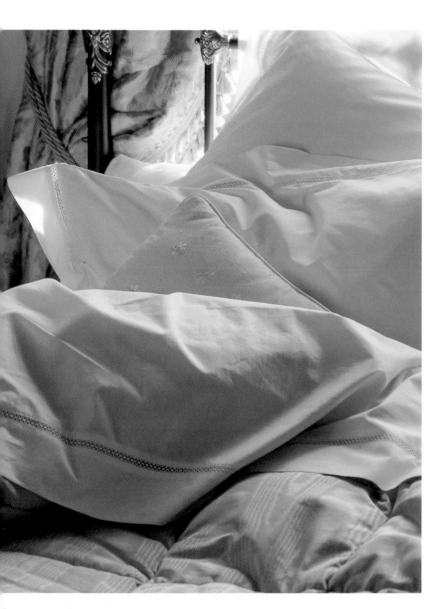

The bedroom is the least public room in the home, yet we spend one third of our lives there. It is fundamental to our sense of well-being, but has been disregarded for centuries when thinking of the home as a whole. It is often the last room we get round to decorating, yet it can be the one place where key moments of our lives occur. It may be the setting for birth or death, relaxation, lovemaking, eating, retreating, taking naps, working, or just thinking. No other room offers such a complete reflection of the human experience or of our sense of self.

The idea of a bedroom as a retreat, a room away from the rest of the home in which we can relax, sleep and revive the spirit is a notion whose appeal grows as the demands of modern life leave little space for quiet calm, contemplation and escape. As the amount of time devoted to sleep diminishes, so the importance given to creating a calm and quiet space seems to increase exponentially.

Nowadays the simple bliss of deep sleep in a bedroom that suits your need for comfort and style, whether it is primarily one of classical elegance, country simplicity or colourful exoticism, is high on the wish-list of modern life. Designing and decorating a bedroom has gradually assumed more importance, on a par with choosing a new kitchen or revamping a living room. It is also a space in

LEFT

*Surrounding
yourself with
crisp cotton
square pillows
and decorative
cushions creates
an instant feeling
of warmth and
invitation.*

RIGHT *A well-
proportioned
bedroom benefits
from the placing
of a beautifully
crafted brass bed
in the centre of
the room, giving
the bed an
important visual
prominence that
influences the
decoration of
the room.*

the house that you can call your own and where you can indulge individual tastes. In Ancient Egypt the socially advantaged spent their nights on elaborate wooden constructions, carved into fantastic animal forms. The legs were shaped into those of lions and other animals, and the wood decorated with vivid, intricate paintwork often inlaid with chased gold and ivory. These beds were very important status symbols, and were understood to have travelled to the grave with their owners.

The Romans and Greeks viewed their beds as places at the centre of social life. They received guests, entertained and even ate on their *klines* (hence the origin of the word 'recline'). These were elegant spare beds softened with a thin loosely stuffed mattress made of rough sacking on which people lounged during the day. At night a small bolster was added as a pillow. The first luxury beds of the Roman Empire were wooden frames decorated in gold, silver or bronze, with mattresses generously filled with reeds, hay, wool or feathers.

By the thirteenth century, the idea of individual beds had been forgotten, with servants and their employers sleeping in the same space. Servants would often retire to a corner, or else bed down in straw near the animals for warmth. For the rest of the household, straw-filled hemp and fustian mattresses would be unfurled and scattered at random on the floor of the great hall, as close as possible to the fire. Heads of affluent households would sometimes retire to a bower, a wooden hut separated from the main building, which was sparsely furnished with a mattress and basic coverlets.

LEFT *The combination of a chunky brass bedstead and mosquito net set against a chalky blue wall creates a romantic atmosphere.*

During the Renaissance, people still slept in twos and threes for warmth. Sir Thomas More's daughters slept on a single truckle bed in the same room as their father, and servants slept at the foot of their masters' and mistresses' bed, on pull-out trundles lined with straw mattresses. In the sixteenth century a separate room for sleeping became more widespread. Once chimneys were invented, the need to cluster around a sole source of heat diminished.

ABOVE *A formal wooden bed placed in a panelled room is a traditional way of embracing comfort and intimacy.*

ABOVE *New four-poster beds incorporate classic design elements such as barley-twist posts, with modern comfort and style through handmade mattresses and careful decorative detailing.*

RIGHT *This ethnic interpretation of the classic posted bed suggests low-level informal living.*

In Tudor times, the bedchamber and its one dominant feature, the bed, assumed great social significance as an investment as important as a car or boat is today. The main bed in any house was an indicator of social standing. Rich householders often spent more on their bed than on anything else in the house. The bed was designed to be dismantled and transported from one country house to another as a potent symbol of rank.

Because the nobility moved home frequently, bedrooms were quite sparsely furnished, with maybe a blanket box for storing clothes and linens as the only additional free-standing piece. Instead, wall hangings provided significant (and transportable) decorative elements. The affluent had intricately sewn tapestries, while poorer households made do with painted cloths. Sometimes the hangings were made from the same fabric as the bed hangings, while Elizabethan homes often had ornately painted wooden panelling on the walls. Under Elizabeth I, bed decoration developed, and half testers and canopies became stylish adjuncts to the frame itself. They were designed to be removable and transportable, in the same way as the bed itself, and provided an additional gauge of wealth, according to the value of the fabrics used. Today, the sheer amount of fabric needed to create a half-tester is a major investment in itself and is not designed to be transported elsewhere once in place.

Although testers and canopies were first introduced into the homes of royalty and statesmen, they gradually filtered down to less grand houses and have endured in popularity. They were traditionally used to frame a bed visually while

providing a means of enclosing and warming the sleeping space. Bed drapes were useful for privacy, keeping out cold draughts and insects, and adding an extra decorative dimension to the bedroom. Testers were attached to the ceiling with chains or ropes so they could be easily removed. Later, the four-poster bed became popular for its integral bed drapes.

The significance of the bedchamber increased during the sixteenth and seventeenth centuries, and royalty took to receiving distinguished guests in their bedchambers. This tradition reached grandiose proportions during the reign of Louis XIV, who spent much of his time in bed. Corridors and rooms leading to the grand bedchamber assumed ever-increasing levels of opulence and the

RIGHT *Dressing a brass bed with plump white pillows and a gorgeous satin eiderdown conjures romance and indulgence.*

BELOW *Bedside tables are important for storage and also tying together the decorative elements in a bedroom.*

ABOVE *Clean lines and simple bed posts make this metal bed frame suited to traditional settings, but it would be equally at home in a modern interior.*

supremely ornate chamber dripped with gold trimmings, heavy brocaded drapes and a bed of gargantuan dimensions. In addition, Louis XIV was said to own 413 beds, many as ostentatious as this one. Other European royalty and aristocracy copied his flamboyant style.

The Elizabethan tradition was to make the bedchamber a welcoming and restful place. Pine cones were burned on

the fire to sweeten the air and copper warming pans placed in beds. We can only guess at the extent of bed bugs and other undesirables in rooms that were not well ventilated, heavy with fabric and thick with fire smoke, so scent in all its forms was important. Pillows stuffed with lavender and rosemary aided relaxation and are often used today for the same purpose. Even farmhouses possessed a 'best bed', which was often a modest four-poster, and ordinary households now ran to a separate bedchamber, even if it were small and more a passageway than a room.

The bed was such a symbolic piece of domestic life that it was often a major item in wills. Shakespeare left his 'best bed' to his daughter, Susannah, while his wife Anne Hathaway, received only the second-best bed.

By the end of the seventeenth century the four-poster had emerged as a fashionable alternative to canopied beds and it remains popular today. Daniel Marot, architect to William of Orange, pioneered the idea of decorating a room as a unity, with the bed-curtain fabric echoed on the chairs and dressing table and at the windows. Such a level of coordination is still considered to define a traditional approach to bedroom decoration and, despite going in and out of fashion, remains an appealing option.

During the eighteenth century, the idea of decorating a bedchamber in coordinating fabrics, upholstery and the newly invented wallpaper led to the introduction of dedicated pieces of furniture to complement this visual richness. Night tables appeared as early bedside tables, with compartments to hide the chamber pot. Washstands and basins appeared. At the beginning of the nineteenth

LEFT *Spare elegance in the form of a simple bed frame that includes filigree-like wrought ironwork is complemented by a luscious red throw and crisp white pillows.*

RIGHT *The sinuous curves of an Empire bed show why this style has never gone out of fashion.*

FAR RIGHT *A new version of the classic sleigh bed looks at home in a country-house room.*

century bedrooms were moved from the ground floor to the first floor, with privacy now an integral part of the room. Bedrooms became the places for private retreat that they remain today. The day bed, once a place of social intercourse in the eighteenth-century boudoir, became a chaise longue often placed at the end of a bed.

Empire style originated in Paris. Between 1800 and 1820 Emperor Napoleon was keen to rekindle the grand lifestyle of Imperial Rome and embraced the clean-lined look with generous quantities of drapes enclosing solid wooden beds, day beds and chaise longues. Probably the most celebrated bed of this period belonged to Mme Récamier, wife of an affluent Parisian banker, whose bedchamber was designed by the influential French architect Charles Percier. The room came to be regarded as the apogee of French Empire style and Napoleon was so impressed that he commissioned Percier on several subsequent occasions. The style spread across Europe to

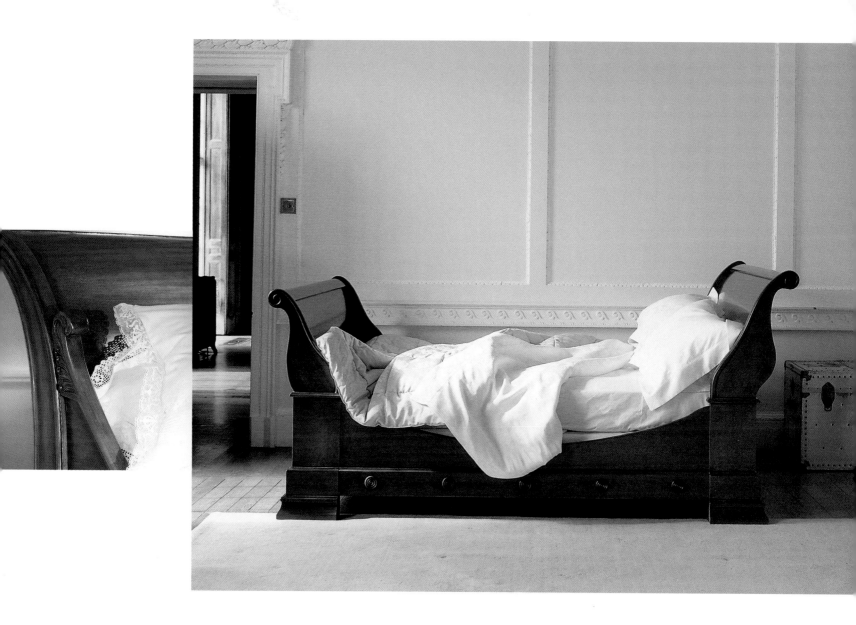

Germany, the Netherlands, Spain, Italy and Russia, and remained in vogue for several decades, especially in Italy. It was known as neoclassical style in America, since it drew much visual reference from Greek and Roman lines.

After Empire came Biedermeier, an Austrian and German tradition of pared-down furniture and bedrooms that evolved from 1815 to the middle of the century. It was characterized by a simple classicism, and came to be considered as the epitome of middle-class contentment.

Biedermeier beds were made from fruitwoods or yew, maple, ash and walnut, and their design often included arches, pediments, columns and wreaths. The bed itself was the centrepiece of the room, since bedroom layouts became more simplified, almost stark. Parquet floors formed a plain stage for these bold yet simple beds and furniture. The style remains fairly minimal in appearance, even to modern eyes, which explains why Biedermeier beds are highly prized today.

ABOVE *The architect and designer Charles Rennie Mackintosh created bedrooms where geometrics were integral to the design, such as these twin beds in a simple symmetrical setting.*

It was not long before the Victorian era of excess arrived, filling the bedroom with numerous pieces of heavy furniture such as tallboys (upright storage pieces that combined chests of drawers with cupboards), shortboys (companion low-level pieces) and fussy dressing tables draped in fabric. The predominant decorative style remained ostentatious and overblown until William Morris

RIGHT *A modern version of the lit à la polonaise, this minimal four-poster iron framework displays a smart elegance yet encloses a simple divan bed.*

and the Arts and Crafts Movement began to introduce some restraint. Once brass bed frames and pocket-sprung mattresses appeared during the late 1800s, a sense of calm emerged in the bedroom, with a new emphasis on materials and simplicity as found in the work of Morris, Sir Edwin Lutyens, Charles Rennie Mackintosh and Carl Larsson in Sweden. The woodwork was often painted white and embellished with simple floral decoration or, in the case of Mackintosh, graphic motifs, to lighten the mood. Rugs became lighter in tone and more graphic in design, while window coverings were much reduced. Swags, drapes and pelmets of heavy velvet were replaced with cotton and ticking. This clean simplicity is popular again with a generation pressed for time. Contemporary iron beds look to tradition for their form but are entirely modern in their decorative style. Duvets rather than blankets dress the bed and enable easy upkeep. Bedlinen is predominately in pale, plain fabrics rather than ornate brocades, simple checks rather than busy patterns. A pared-down approach to furniture elsewhere in the room allows the bed to dictate the look of the space, whether it is in a country cottage, a formal traditional home or an urban loft.

Whether your decorative preferences lean towards rustic charm, urban minimalism or Eastern exoticism, this book will help you enhance your personal space by detailing the origins of each style and suggesting elements for creating the look so that your bedroom can become a place of self-expression and revitalization, allowing you space and time for quality rest and sleep.

All men whilst they are awake are in one common world; but each of them, when he is asleep, is in a world of his own.

PLUTARCH, c.50–c.120

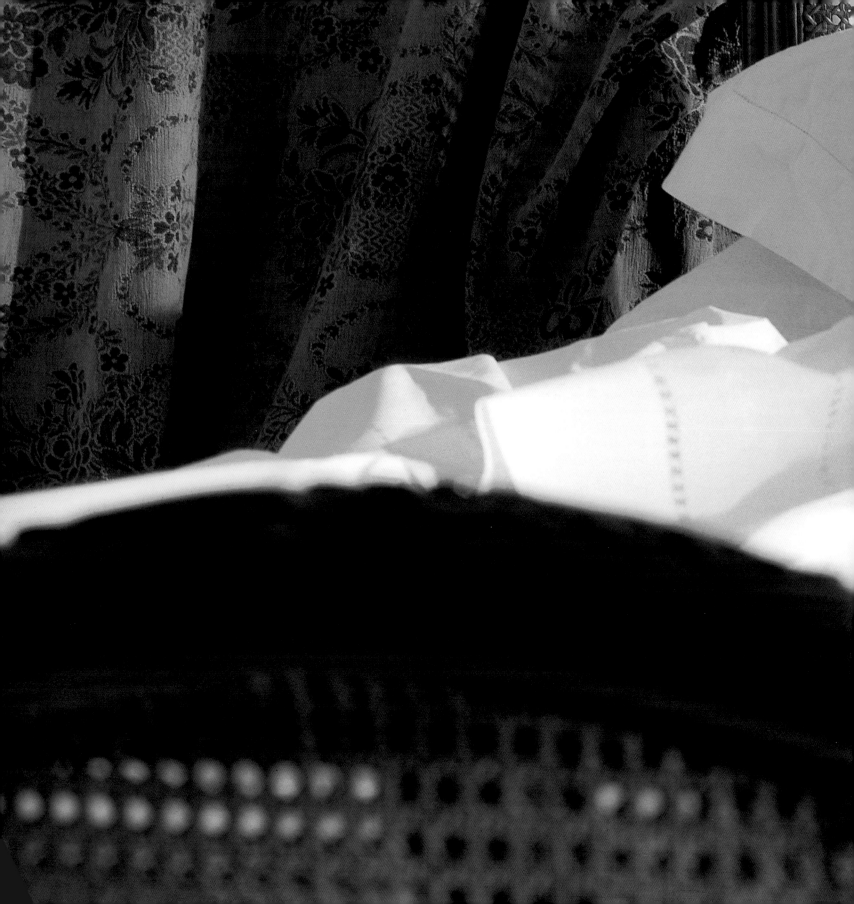

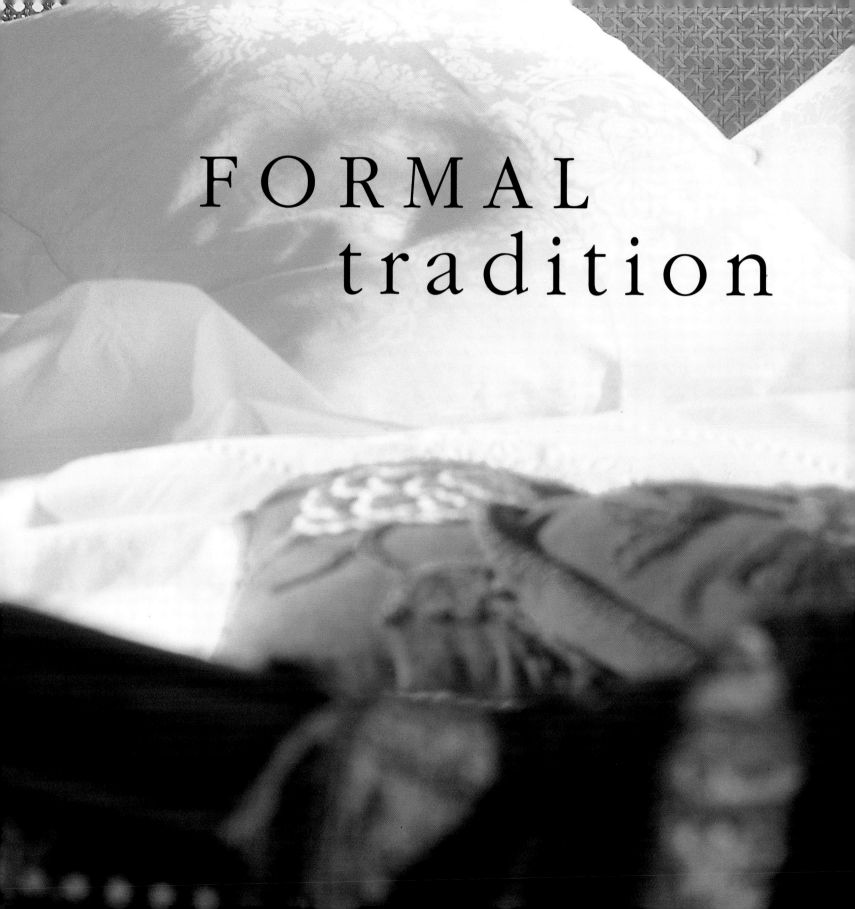

FORMAL
tradition

God bless the inventor of sleep, the cloak that covers all men's thoughts, the food that cures all hunger... The balancing weight that levels the shepherd with the king and the simple with the wise.

MIGUEL DE CERVANTES, 1547–1616

Beds that reflect rich tradition, classic formality and simple lines are as popular today as they were at their conception. The sleek curves of a mahogany Biedermeier, the pleasing simplicity of an iron bedstead and the clean contours of an American post-bed work in settings as diverse as country cottages, urban lofts, small-space apartments and grand family homes.

The notion of formal tradition in the bedroom is a powerful one. It encompasses a range of decorative styles that evolved from Tudor times onwards, when a room solely devoted to sleeping first came into use. Initially, it was only in grand country houses that such a space became a necessity rather than a luxury, but eventually even the most modest of dwellings incorporated a

RIGHT *An early American posted bed traditionally included a fabric canopy and valance. At the bottom of the bed a wooden linen box is both useful and decorative.*

LEFT *This neoclassical bedroom includes a bed whose high headboard and footboard provide a sense of protection for the occupants.*

bedroom. More than any other bedroom styles, formal tradition relies on historical accuracy for its inspiration and reference. Ornately carved four-posters with brocade hangings, smooth sculptural Empire day beds and half-tester bed frames heavily embellished with fabric trimmings all have traditional roots, even when reinterpreted with a modern twist. Wrought-iron four-posters look unmistakably modern yet derive their form from sixteenth-century models, while contemporary day beds, simply styled in cherrywood or wicker, evoke the elegance of traditional upholstered chaises longues. History is never far away from such modern interpretations of classic forms, and many period styles are reproduced in homes where the owners have a passion for one particular epoch, or the architecture dictates a sympathy for one style.

Recent bedroom design has incorporated a merging of old and new, employing an innovative approach to mixing traditional beds and furniture with contemporary decorative accessories. Painted period furniture teamed with solid wooden beds; reconditioned chandeliers and formal bedside lights against a background of modern low-voltage halogen lighting; iron four-posters placed in a loft bedroom. Such surprising juxtapositions no longer jar the senses, but are seen as sympathetic ensembles that display a pragmatic appreciation of history.

Achieving formal tradition in a modern setting is often a question of allowing the bed to dominate the room and leaving the rest of the room to fall into line, coordinating furniture or mixing elements in an eclectic way. Bedlinen will also help to move the look in one direction or another.

LEFT *A superb neoclassical Empire day bed is framed with luxurious silk drapes in duck-egg blue, edged with gilt fabric and fringing.*

RIGHT *This traditionally shaped sleigh bed fits neatly into a contemporary setting where smooth polished surfaces set the decorative tone overall.*

traditional beds

Formal traditional beds whose shape and design evoke particular historic periods or decorative styles are still phenomenally popular today. Often their classic forms have been reinterpreted and redesigned to meet the modern demand for flexible sizing, comfortable high-quality mattresses, fine materials and superlative crafts-manship. Nowadays you can sleep on a traditional-looking four-poster or Empire bed while benefiting from modern comforts and conveniences.

The four-poster bed is an endearing and romantic concept. Once the exclusive preserve of medieval aristoc-racy, it is now completely democratized and much more of an inspirational piece of furniture, especially sought after in hotels and hideaways. Intricately carved and sturdy in the extreme, early four-posters from the sixteenth century were so grand and generously proportioned that it must have been difficult to leave them. From such a welcoming, enclosed space there was little motivation to venture out of the bedroom. The name 'four-poster' applies to all types of bed that incorporate four posts with a canopy or tester that completely covers the bed area. Striking and domi-nant, they are really best saved for large and grand bedrooms because their size can throw the proportions of an average bedroom.

Truckle or trundle beds were originally a medieval Gothic invention. A trundle, which is a pull-out unit on

LEFT *A luxurious four-poster with intricate posts and a deep pelmet of silver grey and dark claret looks gloriously indulgent in a formal setting.*

rollers or casters that slides under the bed when not in use, contains an additional mattress. They were traditionally fixed (often to small-scale beds) for children or servants to sleep on. They were also a common bed in colonial and early American homes, especially Shaker and Amish communities. Useful as guest beds as far back as the

ABOVE *Traditional American post-beds of the nineteenth century were often fitted with lace canopies over the wooden framework.*

*And so home again,
staying nowhere,
and then up to her
chamber, there to
talk with pleasure of
this day's passages
and so to bed.*

SAMUEL PEPYS'S DIARY
4 MARCH 1668

seventeenth century, they were mentioned by Samuel Pepys. They are reproduced today with unsqueaky trundles and in fine materials that stand up to heavy use.

Canopy beds derived their name from the Greek word meaning 'a net to keep out gnats'. The canopies formed a fabric roof over a four-posted bed that was most often supported at each corner, or suspended from above. Usually draped over a piece of furniture, it offered both decoration and protection. In eighteenth-century France, many variations of canopies were given individual names. A *lit à colonnes* had a canopy supported on four visible wooden columns, whereas a *lit à la polonaise* was made from curved iron supports that formed a dome that was swathed in fabric. An unsupported canopy that was shorter than the bed itself was known as a *lit d'ange*, while canopies attached to the wall behind or to the ceiling were *lits à la duchesse*. Still more variations evolved in France, England and America.

Beds with canopies are a softer version of the four-poster. Invariably inviting, they can be made more romantic by adding muslin curtains beneath heavier outer curtains, and less formal by using tactile fabrics such as organza and satin.

Testers are flat wooden canopies that lie over and above a bedstead, supported by four posts, or by two at one or the other end of the bed. The French medieval word *testière* indicates how old this type of bed is. Originally testers were ornately panelled and carved, forming small roofs over four-posted Tudor and Stuart bedheads. They were gradually replaced by a wooden framework that was

RIGHT *This grand brass lit à la polonaise is hugely appealing in a baronial setting with silk drapes and an embroidered bed hanging, but would look at home in a more modestly furnished room.*

LEFT *Wooden beds with matching bedside tables always create a pleasing harmony of material and colour. Here, large pillows and a steely grey eiderdown enhance the comfort factor.*

BELOW AND CENTRE *A scrolled-end Empire bed with a star motif at each corner of its wooden base provides graphic definition in a neutral space.*

draped heavily with fabric and cocooned with valances for a softer appeal. By the mid-eighteenth century, testers were more likely to be a small wooden cornice fitted with a fabric valance and curtains, but were neat, elegant and luxurious in appearance. These beds look most at home in traditionally decorated period bedrooms.

Empire beds are shaped like wooden sleigh beds (also known as *lits bateaux*) and incorporate elegant carved headboards and footboards of equal proportions, whose scrolled or roundelled ends are delicately contoured. At first, the solid wood was painted or lacquered in black, then ornately decorated with painted neoclassical figures and garlands. Later versions were simply made from mahogany or cherrywood and left unadorned. The classic Empire-style bed is low and usually set against a wall or in an alcove, with only one main side exposed.

Sleigh beds were a nineteenth-century American adaptation of the Empire bed and were also known as scroll beds from the early twentieth century. They are simplified versions of the Empire bed and are enduring classics, produced in a variety of woods and styles. They work well in both traditional and modern bedrooms as their curved outlines soften the room, especially if the wood has an interesting patina.

Boat beds were not, as their name suggests, floating palaces of sleep, but beds placed in an alcove, with only one long side showing. Popular during the French Empire and English Restoration as well as in early America, they were often made in light-coloured woods with contrasting wooden marquetry and raised up on a large, step-like

base. Today, they are ideal for guest rooms and also as adaptable children's beds. They are generally made from solid, good-quality wood to withstand constant use.

Other formal styles that remain popular today include solid wooden bedsteads, either posted or with headboards and footboards made from pine, mahogany, oak and walnut. These formal rustic beds are often quite high off the ground and have a natural, enveloping warmth about them. Solid panelled headboards and footboards evoke French and Italian Renaissance beds, especially if they include carved detailing. Preserve them with a rich, natural wood polish such as beeswax and you introduce a sensuous dimension, too.

Among the earliest forms of multi-functional furniture from which contemporary design takes inspiration is the day bed, first seen in the salons of Ancient Rome and Greece, on which noble people sat to receive guests, eat, drink and sleep. By the mid-seventeenth century, day beds were being placed in a closet, off the bedchamber, for women to receive admirers or simply to relax.

FAR LEFT *Solid wood headboards and footboards make a striking shape in the middle of a bedroom, their fine legs lifting the frame up off the ground and creating an elegant formality in the room.*

LEFT *Canework goes in and out of fashion but never loses its effortlessly comfortable style. First used in the seventeenth century, it was popular again at the beginning of the twentieth century, when Orientalism was at its height, and again at the beginning of the twenty-first, with its preoccupation with natural materials and organic forms.*

RIGHT *A classic chaise longue transcends the whims of fashion and finds favour with any decorative style.*

The chaise longue was a Victorian innovation, taking the simple day bed and adding a curved headboard and side arm. It was placed at the bottom of the bed and used by the lady of the house for drying her hair in front of the fire or reclining while receiving visitors. It is ideal for 'public' areas of a home, such as hallways and living rooms, where people can snatch a few moments of comfort. In a bedroom, it adds an elegant touch and is useful as a temporary storage space, appealing as both a piece of furniture and a decorative statement.

And mighty proud I am (and ought to be, thankful to God Almighty) that I am able to have a spare bed for my friends.

SAMUEL PEPYS'S DIARY
8 AUGUST 1666

ABOVE *A handpainted bedstead with canework panels at either end is beautifully complemented by a fabric half-tester above the headboard.*

RIGHT *Luscious ochre silk fabric hangs from a corona to overarch a smart Knole-style day bed. Bolsters complete the air of dramatic formality.*

bed drapery and dressing

Bed drapery and dressing have a rich tradition that connects in with numerous different decorative styles and types of bed. The first testers appeared during medieval times and were suspended from the ceiling with hooks, ropes or chains. Later, solid wooden structures were permanently fixed to the walls and luxurious bed drapes suspended from them. Popular early fabrics included embroidered red velvet, worsted and heavy damask silks with rich trimmings for grander interiors, while modest homes made do with simple cotton drapes. Bed curtains often had an inner curtain of sheer muslin or lace, used to deter insects as well as to present a softer visual edge for the bed's inhabitants. Often heavy curtains were removed in favour of lighter fabrics and more summery colours when the season changed. However, bed bugs must have thrived in such fabric-laden environments.

Bed curtains were frequently made to link in with the handwoven tapestries or painted cloths that were used as decoration on the walls. In most cases the quality of the fabric used for bed dressing was more important than the quality of materials used to construct the tester or canopy frame. It was seen, like the bed itself, as an indicator of social standing.

The wide variety of testers and canopies is firmly linked to the posted and the four-poster bed. Early posted beds were more likely to have two posts at the foot end, with a

conventional tall bedhead at the other, on which simple drapes, or a tester, were supported. Towards the end of the seventeenth century, English and French beds of this type each had a distinct identity. The French versions tended to be of a square shape with simple wooden valances (the side rails that run above and around the top of the bed), overlaid with simple drapery. English versions tended to have elaborately carved valances that were left on view. In the United States mahogany and cherrywood beds were simply embellished with four simple poles and draped with lacework.

Pelmets and valances add formality to posted or canopied beds, particularly if finished with traditional fringing or trimming. Floral and patterned fabrics edged with plain borders and designed to coordinate with window dressings give a neat effect. Today's interpretations of canopies and half-testers tend to be streamlined versions, in both styles of beds and choice of fabrics. Simple striped runs of cotton or ticking draped simply over a metal-framed bed, or discreet coronas of floral fabric gathered over a half-corona are more in keeping with modern traditional style. In these contemporary forms, bed drapes and canopies have never disappeared altogether from the domestic bedroom. Muslin drapes

RIGHT *Exquisite classical detailing gives this baroque bedchamber an air of grand sophistication. Pale blue and gold were very popular in eighteenth century French decoration.*

remain very popular, as some form of enclosure continues to be seen as a romantic, as well as practical, decorative solution. It is merely the style that has changed. There is simply not the time or inclination to make, maintain and dust around huge swathes of chintz or velvet. Interior fashions also come and go at such a rate that there is a reluctance to make a huge investment in luxury fabric that may date easily. The bed as a status symbol has become a piece of furniture whose priorities are generous proportions, flexibility, fine design and, above all, comfort.

TOP *Silk sheets are the ultimate choice for seductive bedlinen.*

CENTRE *A brocaded throw imparts traditional opulence to any bed.*

BELOW *Some bed manufacturers supply ranges of bedlinen to complement their particular styles of beds. These rich cotton sheets are embellished with embroidered scrollwork.*

formal bedroom styles

A number of formal decorative styles can be employed to create a crisp, traditional bedroom that flirts with history but is not a slave to it. Decorating a bedroom with formal tradition in mind is a question of pinpointing an era with which you are comfortable and which works in your bedroom space, then deciding which key elements to use to achieve your scheme.

The bed is more often than not the main starting point, since no bedroom can function without its bed. Choosing fabric and bedlinen is probably the next most important element, as window coverings and bed dressing are important to the overall look. Clothes storage and lighting can be treated in a traditional manner by incorporating free-standing pieces such as antique armoires, scrolled chests of drawers, or painted and distressed period chests and cupboards. By adding elements such as glass chandeliers, iron wall sconces and solid bedside lights with pleated shades, formal lighting can transform the decorative focus of a bedroom. Modern convenience may be secured by fitting dimmer switches to antique pendant lights and inserting recessed low-voltage spotlights into the ceiling. Wallpaper is important, too, as is flooring.

Creating a mix-and-match period scheme is one way of introducing a glorious statement bed into a room where existing or heirloom furniture is already established. The celebrated interior designer John Fowler was an expert on

BELOW *Victorian bedlinen was not always adorned with lace. This crisp linen set includes punched striped designs for a graphic edging.*

ABOVE *A royal-blue and gold throw conjures the Louis XIV era of French decoration.*

RIGHT *This generously proportioned sleigh bed, designed along traditional lines but incorporating up-to-date comfort, suits its traditional setting, and is dressed with red and green brocade cushions.*

eighteenth-century decoration and in the process of restoring some English National Trust houses became closely associated with the English country-house look that was popular for much of the twentieth century, from the 1930s onwards. He later went on to become part of Colefax and Fowler, the decoration company that still upholds the pleasure of chintz and tradition in interior design and style.

Other formal approaches to bedrooms often included coordinating fabrics on bedlinen, curtains and upholstery for elegance. Regency style is popular with those who prefer a country-house aesthetic. Solid wooden bedheads placed against luxurious vertically striped wallpaper in deep two-tone shades of bottle green, claret and midnight blue look smart and club-like. Colours tend to be deep and strong, with bedlinen consisting of crisp white sheets and heavy bedspreads.

For a feminine rococo elegance, large gilt mirrors and satin bed curtains or bedspreads in baby blue and a hint of dusky pink will tilt a scheme towards the eighteenth century without your having to invest too heavily in antique furniture. If you have any family heirlooms, storing clothes in antique armoires and panelled chests is decorative, but it can be difficult to dispense with the added space that built-in wardrobes offer, unless a small dressing area can be tucked into the bedroom, an en suite bathroom or a nearby landing.

In many bedrooms, people often choose comfort over convenience and lay thick-pile carpets or rugs. However, the bedroom is one room above all where dust should be

LEFT *Cushions made from panels of rich brocades and chintz help tie a decorative scheme together.*

RIGHT *Recalling a feminine boudoir, this Empire-style room is painted yellow, a popular colour of the time. The lit bateau is crowned with a white silk corona, whose fabric is repeated at the window and finished with a swagged pelmet of rich blue silk and silver fringing.*

FAR LEFT *Upholstered headboards can supply much of the fabric decoration in the bedroom. This subtle, striped fabric echoes the scrolled Empire lines of a French antique bedstead.*

LEFT *Rich red fabric tones with the natural qualities of leather and carved wood are an arresting combination.*

BELOW *A modern version of the classic day bed looks perfectly at home in a period setting.*

kept to an absolute minimum. Natural matting such as sisal, seagrass and jute is a good solution for achieving this. It looks similar to the medieval matting that was laid under formal four-posters and provides a natural and neutral material for any decorating style, while also acknowledging modern preferences for more eco-friendly decorating options.

Painted, stained or stripped floorboards are also sensible, as they are easy to clean and the look can be softened with small but luxurious rugs and runners.

Many formal styles retain instant appeal to modern eyes. While the fascination for Victorian and grand country style, may have diminished, the past continues to inspire bedroom designers and bed producers. It is more usual now to combine antique and traditional elements with contemporary features in an eclectic mix of old and new for a feeling of comfort and relaxed elegance.

COUNTRY chic

The essence of country decorating is, above all, modesty and understatement. Country bedrooms especially should be places of simplicity, subtle romanticism and appealing utility – a matter of mood rather than statement, a way of life rather than ostentatious display. It is here that time slows down, for life can be measured by the rising sun rather than by the harsh tones of an alarm clock. A soft elegant approach to decoration means the country bedroom is a place of refuge, renewal and inspiration.

The cheerful image of a rose-bowered country cottage is as potent now as it always has been. There is no doubt that a rural home that carefully displays its fine outer layers of climbing roses, lilac, wisteria and clematis draped around a painted door, the air suffused with the scent of potted herbs, is an image that never fails to give pleasure and a sense of peace. It is a picture associated with escape, contentment, replenishment and a simple life. The notion of living an uncomplicated existence in a small cottage whose enclosing walls both cocoon and invite has a reassuring quality. Bringing the outside in, by displaying home-grown flowers and greenery in the bedroom and elsewhere, reinforces the natural connection.

Country bedrooms demand understated furnishings in a relaxed atmosphere that relies on the decorative interest of natural materials and textures. Making the most of natural light always pays dividends in the country, where it is often more plentiful than in urban locations. Positioning a bed so that it catches the morning sun is an easy way to optimize the start of each day. Emphasizing the natural elements of the countryside means keeping furnishings

It was such a lovely day, I thought it was a pity to get up.

W. SOMERSET MAUGHAM

1874–1965

LEFT *A simple divan with classic country lacey bedlinen fits exactly in a charming tiny white bedroom. Natural light floods through tiny gothic shutters.*

LEFT *The classic Mediterranean bedroom style centres on painted shutters and woodwork complemented by a simple brass bed.*

RIGHT *In old cottages, where the walls speak volumes, all that is required is a simple divan and bedspread.*

light and airy. Simple glass vases filled with freshly picked flowers and foliage will imbue the bedroom with gentle scent, old furniture spruced up with a wash of white paint conveys a sense of informality, and a bed dressed to please finishes the picture with a welcome flourish.

Simplicity is central to the modest charm of a country bedroom. Whitewashed walls punctuated with dark wooden beams offer a natural framework for light-painted bedsteads; brass beds or wooden sleigh beds curve at either end to create a feeling of enclosure. Country bedrooms look best painted in pale clear tones, as heavy colours can be too intense for relaxation and often over accentuate the delightful irregularities of timeworn walls. Soft duck-egg blues, pale citrus and variations of white and beige are all comfortable shades that create a subtle background against which a mix of textures and materials will harmonize effortlessly. Other fundamentals include a sensitive eye for painted furniture and for period pieces,

LEFT *In a country barn conversion, a simple iron four-poster frame is studded at each corner with pale green wooden posts hung with tab-headed curtains in olive green and white.*

ABOVE *On the English Cornish coast, a seaside retreat is decorated in shades of white. The only interruption to the colour is a wooden chest of drawers underneath the window.*

and a light touch when it comes to fabric. Combining these elements will make a space where simple comfort and escape evoke a sense of the country – an achievable dream.

Classic country bedrooms encompass a wide variety of styles, from the organic, earthy appeal of hillside log cabins and folk-art-inspired painted furniture, to bright Mediterranean colour, all-white romantic boltholes, the laid-back charm of rural France and a contemporary aesthetic known as 'Modern Country'.

Rustic style does not mean fussy detailing. Often a modern outlook applied to a period country house creates a pleasing symphony of old and new, an easy marriage of materials – battered beams against smooth new oak or beech beds, distressed bedheads coupled with crisp white linen and a textured throw. Floorboards stripped and treated with a sympathetic wash, stain or varnish can also make a variety of decorative statements. Painted chequerboard designs or simple applied borders both evoke a folk tradition and give a modern edge. For a more romantic atmosphere, whitewashed boards provide a neutral base. Boards stained a deep brown or black will complement dark timbers, while polished parquet or beech strip flooring lends instant contemporary appeal.

Whatever the geographical location, country decorating endures because it transcends fashion and creates a restrained, comfortable retreat for city dwellers and their rural counterparts. Despite constant reinterpretation, the rural idyll is still thriving and inviting.

country
beds

The contemporary cottage bed needs to be comfortable and welcoming. The smooth and varied textures of natural wood are in easy sympathy with the shabby chic of many old cottages, as are traditional polished brass bedsteads. Since their introduction at the end of the nineteenth century, they have proved to be endlessly appealing. Forged metal bedsteads in traditional and modern designs

BELOW LEFT *A Swedish-style wooden day bed converts easily into a sleeping space.*

BELOW *Country iron and brass bedsteads are reproduced in a variety of colours and materials.*

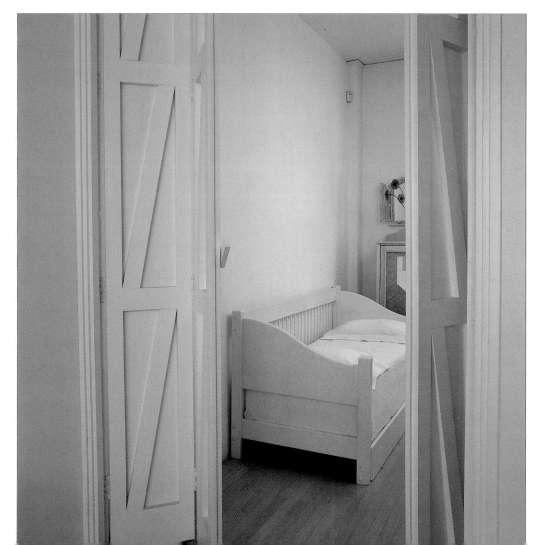

RIGHT *Rustic Celtic beds were often very simple. This one is accompanied by a traditional nineteenth-century wooden rocker cot.*

also suit country schemes, their clean lines contrasting with the soft, irregular contours of old buildings.

Metal-framed beds, usually of iron or brass tubing, first became popular in the mid-nineteenth-century, while wrought-iron headboards were familiar even earlier in Mediterranean countries; cast iron appeared in decorative designs in France, America and Spain during the 1800s. They lend themselves well to the huge variety of quilts, blankets and throws associated with country style.

From its early peasant roots, the country bed was, of necessity, simple and modest. A wooden bed supported either a simple hessian sacking base or rows of tightly tied ropes that supported a mattress. The term 'sleep tight' arose from the need to tighten the ropes every so often. Once brass beds became widespread, they were often used for servants in attic rooms. Their frames lacked complicated embellishment or decoration, so were very easy to maintain and clean.

LEFT *This traditional wooden bed is very similar to the one immortalized in Vincent van Gogh's paintings. Neat, classic and comfortable.*

RIGHT *In a converted chapel, an informal Mediterranean aim is achieved with painted shutters, stone flooring, a red rug and a wooden bedstead popular of a kind in France, Italy and Spain during the nineteenth century.*

Iron bedsteads have the easy simplicity that suits the utilitarian virtues of rural living. In simple country crofts, such as those in Ireland, France and Scotland (where they were called 'black houses' because they had no windows, to preserve warmth), beds were often built into a niche in the wall, framed in wood and covered with thick woven fabric for additional warmth.

Wooden beds were often painted to disguise their uneven surfaces and to cheer up the spartan rooms in which they were placed. Painted bed frames are particularly evocative of country style, especially decorated in soft putty colours such as grey, pale blue, buttermilk and primrose. Plain, distressed or adorned with country motifs, the most ordinary of bedframes is transformed into a decorative statement with a coat of paint.

Architects and designers who have given an urban twist to country decorating have discovered that modern divan beds with simple upholstered headboards can work very well in a country setting, their clean lines complementing the basic architectural framework of rural homes. The celebrated minimalist John Pawson has redesigned a barn in Essex in which the architectural beams are the only embellishment. The rest is a white space in which pale beech is used for all the furniture, including the bed.

LEFT *An iron posted bed complete with regal-looking scrollwork fulfils a grand country ideal. The foot board is designed so that opulent bedspreads tuck behind it so as not to detract from the intricate brass pattern.*

RIGHT *A few examples of the immense variety of materials, shapes and finishes for finials and top knobs on classic country beds.*

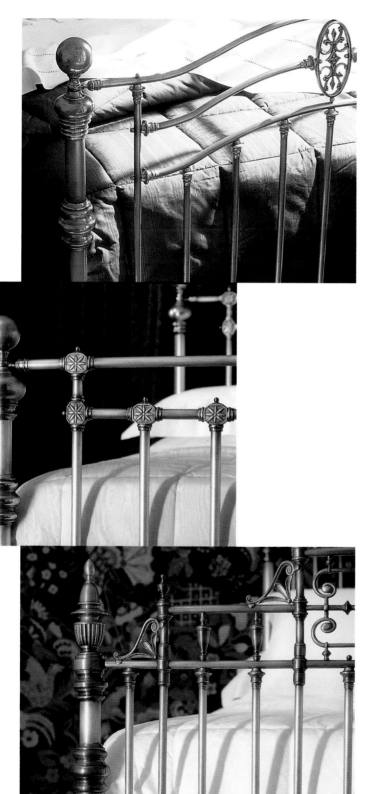

We are such stuff
As dreams are made on,
and our little life
Is rounded with a sleep.

'THE TEMPEST'

WILLIAM SHAKESPEARE,   1564–1616

Divans often look good in converted barns and beamed cottages, where the decorative interest comes from the architecture itself. Placing an overbearing and much-embellished bed in such a setting would detract from the room itself. Tricia Guild, the designer known for her use of strong colour, has toned down the pattern in her Tuscan country home, allowing the natural colours of the surrounding landscape to influence her bedroom colours (broken cobalt blue to reflect the sky, soft lemon-yellow for sunshine), then added only small jolts of pattern to provide subtle decorative flourishes. The beds have simple wrought-iron frames that do not detract from the colours.

The brass bedstead that has become a mainstay of country decorating also evokes a Victorian austerity that somehow suits modestly furnished country homes. Some reproduction brass beds are made with surround frames that fit snugly over a divan base and mattress, allowing space all round the mattress to accommodate a squashy country quilt or bedspread. They also allow any combination of brass headrails and footrails to be added. The traditional Victorian-style bed has an iron framework that supports a bed base and sprung mattress.

dressing the bed

The appeal of a country bedroom decorated with pale, fresh colours and furnished with a bed dressed in understated elegance, then finished off with a simple quilt or bedcover and a textured throw, is irresistibly romantic, blending traditional decoration with natural materials and motifs for a classic style. The contents of a country linen cupboard are often a direct reflection of everything that is good about the countryside. Faded floral eiderdowns, crisp white sheets waiting for use, familiar old blankets and heirloom quilts that straddle several generations are a happy mixture of comfort and style. Add to these lace-edged pillowcases, bolster cushions with striped covers, flat bordered linen cushions, plump woollen throws and slippery satin eiderdowns, faded with use, for a rich variety of country bed dressings.

Climbing into a brass bed that is aired, scented and made up with starchy, pristine white cotton sheets, plump pillows or bolsters is pure joy. Sometimes the hard work involved in laundering 100 per cent cotton sheets and keeping them gleaming white is worth the effort, if only so you can collapse exhausted on them for a night of solid sleep. Equally as comfortable and time consuming, but more luxurious and costly, are linen sheets, whose tactile properties are completely captivating. More contemporary, and certainly more suited to everyday use, are jersey-cotton sheets, recently revived and available in many soft

FAR LEFT *White cotton sheets edged with a linked chain-stitch design and a deep flat border give crisp definition to a country bedstead.*

LEFT *A simple bamboo frame-work forms a headboard to which a muslin panel is attached with fabric bows for femininity. The cream bedlinen is edged and decorated with white borders and motifs to provide texture for the neutral colour scheme.*

LEFT AND ABOVE *Textured throws and lace-edged pillows are perfect for country beds, as are cotton waffle throws and bedlinen in neutral colours. An extra layer of texture always visually warms a space.*

colours such as grey, off-white and blue. Their particularly soft texture provides a luxurious comfort and allows you to climb into bed and feel as though you are snuggling up in a warm fleece, a cosy sensation.

White cotton bedlinen that is machine embroidered or handstitched has an additional decorative element that looks crisp in a pared-down bedroom. Decorated bedlinen works especially well set against simple brass or iron bedsteads that may seem too utilitarian if not softened visually with sympathetic bedlinen.

Country bedrooms are often used for entertaining guests, so a sense of welcome is something to be encouraged. Keep beds freshly laundered and have a stack of soft towels at the ready, together with a room fragrance to breathe life into the space. If the bed is left unmade, place a throw or quilt over it.

country quilts

A handmade quilt is heavily symbolic of the country ethos. Once a vital part of everyday life, it is now more decorative than functional, but its popularity as the epitome of country comfort continues. Embroidered, appliquéd or patchworked, the quilt has the virtue of dual functionality giving both warmth and decoration.

Traditionally a bed quilt was the only element in a country bedroom that was patterned and colourful. As such, it gave much pleasure and became an important part of the decoration of a room. In the United States, quilts were traditionally used to envelop newborn babies, protect valuable belongings in transit, as wall hangings on early settlers' wagons, and of course as winter warmers. During the American Civil War of 1861–5, soldiers were sent off to battle with handmade quilts to provide well-needed warmth. Meanwhile, at home, women made more quilts to auction for food. Quilts from the Amish, Shaker and folk-art tradition have become highly sought-after collectors' pieces. In the north of England, the Durham quilters were equally celebrated.

Among the most beautiful traditional quilts are those created by the religious Amish community, who learnt their sewing skills from non-Amish neighbours in Pennsylvania in the mid-1850s. Despite living a frugal, functional existence in which artifice and decoration were shunned, the Amish created quilts of great beauty and colour.

ABOVE *A classic blue checked quilt is edged with a plain colour and set against floral bedlinen for a truly rustic look.*

LEFT *An appliquéd quilt is crucial for creating a home-spun mood in this bedroom.*

RIGHT *Cotton fabric with small spriggy floral prints in varying sizes is enhanced by machine embroidery.*

Quilts were seen as functional necessities, so detailed attention was given to every aspect of their creation.

Classic quilt designs possess evocative names such as Log Cabin, Diamond in Square, Star of Bethlehem and Tumbling Blocks. Many of them are geometric abstract representations of everyday events and surroundings, since the religious beliefs of the Amish and Mennonite peoples forbade them to produce figurative reproductions of God's creations. The quilts therefore became important means of permissible self-expression. Tumbling Blocks evoked blocks of straw stacked in barns, while the strips in Log Cabins alluded to logs being piled one on top of another to construct a wooden building.

Traditional country quilts were often associated with thrift and recycling. Left-over fabrics from clothes or weaving were cut up and used to form the basis of a repeating pattern or design. Quilters' bees were groups of women who met in each other's homes to sew and talk, often taking months to complete an intricate design that was used to create a wedding quilt or a baby quilt. When a woman married she would have her bed quilt already prepared for her by her friends and family and stored in her 'hope chest'.

These days, throws are equally as popular as quilts. Bed-sized rectangles of fake fur, nubbly waffle blankets in a rich variety of colours and checked cashmere blankets have all become fashionable alternatives to the traditional quilt. However, they will never entirely replace it as the classic bed cover that combines the craft aesthetic with simple elegance.

country bedroom fabrics

In traditional eighteenth-century English country houses, beds were most often free-standing design statements draped in heavy brocade or silk fabric, displaying a more luxurious formality than their modest, peasant counterparts. It was in these grand houses that floral chintz was first popularized during the nineteenth century as *the* bedroom fabric to display. Once coordinated bedlinen, curtains and upholstery had become associated with smart living, the idea really took off. Despite chintz gradually developing staid, safe and uninteresting connotations, floral fabrics have remained undeniably popular for the bedroom, albeit in diluted, less grandiose designs. Nowadays, glamorous rose-bowered fabrics have given way to neat 1950s-style designs, the emphasis placed on utility rather than ostentation.

Sweet pillows, sweetest bed;
A chamber deaf to noise, and blind to light;
A rosy garland, and a weary head.

ALGERNON SIDNEY, 1622–83

LEFT *Rose-decorated chintz is synonymous with the country-house aesthetic that never really goes too far out of fashion, steeped as it is in comfort and reassurance.*

Checked and striped fabrics are very appealing for country settings. They work well at small windows, sit happily alongside naive quilt designs and blend with crisp cotton bedlinen and muslin net curtains. Simple striped banners draped over an iron four-poster frame are a pared-down variation of the traditional post-bed that looks at home in a country setting. Muslin canopies, once the preserve of elegant colonial interiors, also lend natural style to single and double beds, their sense of translucent enclosure gently enticing.

ABOVE *Vintage floral fabrics, both originals and reproductions, are the epitome of country-cottage style. In the classic shades of red, white, pink and blue, they instantly conjure up country flowers and simple living.*

Cabin beds, *lits en niche* (beds built into a wall or alcove), post-beds and tester beds all benefit from some kind of fabric treatment. For country appeal, simple designs such as florals, plains, stripes or checks, and unpretentious fabrics such as cotton, scrim, muslin and ticking work best. Seasonal variations are often more marked in the country. Howling winter winds and rain give way to jewel-bright sunshine and intense heat, so it is practical to accumulate summer and winter curtains, as well as a variety of rugs and bedlinen to cope with all seasons and temperatures.

At the windows, flexible treatments such as loop-headed cotton drapes can be swapped around according to the season, and muslin nets or roller blinds offer privacy without blocking out all the light. Draughts are a consideration in country bedrooms, so choose your curtain fabric according to how much warmth needs to be preserved and how large the windows are. Small, simple casement windows ask for uncomplicated curtains or blinds such as lace panels, pale roller blinds or coloured muslin. Often rural settings mean that you are not overlooked by neighbours, so window treatments can be less formal. A simple muslin drape without a curtain pole may be all that is required. Alternatively a wooden box pelmet can be painted to blend or tone with the walls, and seasonal curtains hung beneath it.

ABOVE *Scalloped edges are often used on bedspreads, pillows and curtain pelmets as a softening device in country-bedroom decoration, while white Irish linen (*RIGHT*) is perfect for preserving a crisp, just-made-up look.*

FAR RIGHT *Checks and stripes have appeared on country fabrics for centuries, in the form of ticking, gingham, striped woven floor runners and candy-coloured stripes. Their popularity seems never to diminish.*

FOLK
art

Of course, I love seven pillows behind me, but physical comfort is never the first thing. I prefer spiritual comfort, by which I mean space, light (natural as well as artificial), contrast of textures, and pure linen. I never look for literal comfort, but for something that allows my mind to rest.

ANDRÉE PUTMAN
(Contemporary interior designer)

Folk-art style encompasses the rich peasant traditions of decorative painting and craftsmanship that go back to the skilled artisans of the eighteenth and nineteenth centuries. The unique beauty of modest materials, carefully decorated with bold colour and pattern, creates a cheerful visual treat that stirs, rather than jars, the senses. Choose from the intricate stencilled floral motifs of the Pennsylvanian Dutch settlers and the glowing colours of Mexican and Mediterranean painted furniture, or the clean, simple lines of Shaker craftsmanship. The raw and chunky woodwork and handwoven textiles of New Mexico and the bedcovers of Appalachia belong to the same story. Folk art is country style gone global, a glorious mix of colour and pattern, floral motifs and vernacular imagery.

Peasant decoration the world over is noted for its spirit of decorative abundance in the face of material deprivation. Traditionally it has been in the most modest homes that an adventurous attitude to decorative painting has transformed an interior. With a rich history of carved and fretworked bedheads, painterly embellishments of naturalistic motifs such as hearts, flowers, oak leaves and feathers, in colours that glow on the gloomiest of days, the tradition is very much alive today.

Vernacular craftsmanship, from carpentry to embroidery, decorative painting and sewing, has been used in bedrooms to great effect. Indeed, peasant style has a remarkable visual similarity, wherever it is in the world: Mexico or Sweden, Latvia or Provence. Colourful and welcoming, folk-art bedrooms are sleeping spaces that are cosy and inviting, artistic and inventive. The bed itself

LEFT *Painted bedsteads are an integral part of the folk tradition. Rich muddy blues, ochres and earthy reds were familiar to the Shakers, while a bright red was used in the Austrian Tyrol, throughout Eastern Europe and also in Scandinavia.*

usually has a high comfort factor, often protected and contained, with handwoven curtains, embroidered drapes or a wooden fretwork frame.

There is something undeniably romantic about enclosed beds. In northern Europe, the tradition of box beds was strong, and many survive today. The Nordic and Celtic countries, with their fierce winters, often used box and cabin beds to keep in heat and protect from draughts. Handwoven woollen drapes provided extra warmth and decorative interest. Carl Larsson, the famed Swedish designer who was inspired as much by the folk tradition as by the Arts and Crafts Movement, designed his own wooden bed and placed it in the centre of his bedroom, painted white and hung with striped drapes designed and made by his wife Karin. Larsson was much influenced by the Swedish eighteenth-century Gustavian tradition, which in turn was a simplification of the overblown French rococo style that had quickly filtered down to the peasant population as an adventurous approach to wood-work and its decoration. Broken and distressed colour was applied to beds, linen cupboards and simple bedside pieces then smartened up with edges painted in gilt cream. The look defined the handcrafted, comfortable atmosphere of folk decoration and its popularity has never diminished.

Motifs are all-important, whether carved into bedheads or applied with paint. In the Austrian Tyrol and New England, heart shapes were carved out of the bedhead for ventilation, but now are purely decorative. Tulips are a legacy from the Dutch settlers in Pennsylvania, while oak leaves symbolize the close links with nature that inspired

travelling decorators. Chunky fretwork decorated with religious scenes was a keynote of New Mexican and Mexican style, and also appeared on Tyrolean beds and cupboards. In Eastern Europe, particularly in Latvia and Russia, elaborate red and white floral designs decorated floor-to-ceiling cabin beds.

There is often a hint of the nomad in folk beds. Think of the traditional Romany caravan, with not a single patch of unpainted wood in its carved fretwork, or the canal boat with built-in bunks, decorated with flowery brushstrokes.

LEFT *Carl and Karin Larsson developed a wholesome, colourful style of decorating at their home, Lilla Hyttnäs, in Sundborn in Sweden. In Karin's bedroom, a built-in bed was tucked into one corner and there was always space for a green-painted child's cot at the other end.*

RIGHT *Clutter and function are happy companions in a traditional Romany caravan, where the bed slots into one end of the space and is crammed with soft red velvets, embroidered curtains and cushions – day bed and sleeping space rolled into one.*

folk bedrooms

Even the most modest peasant bedroom would have some painted furniture to go with the bed. A wooden chest for storing bedlinen, textiles and cushions, often a 'hope chest', would be heavily decorated with floral motifs or written information such as the date of a wedding or betrothal. The decoration of such a box would be carried out over a long time; once finished, it became a prized possession and an enduring, functional piece of furniture. While box beds were the most common form of Swedish peasant bed, more affluent households would also have possessed a four-poster bed with curtains.

In the Austrian Tyrol, dominated by the presence of natural materials such as larch, fir and pine woods, the houses grew 'organically' from the ground and painted decoration was very much the peasant tradition. When a woman married, she presented her husband with a cupboard, bedhead or both. The heart motif is especially popular, carved and labelled with her name and the date of the wedding. Painted linen cupboards are an example of how the folk tradition translates easily from one culture to another. Universally functional, the decorated cupboard is equally at home in Mexico and the Caribbean in rural France and India.

Red is a colour common to a lot of peasant decoration. Cross-stitching in Sweden and Eastern Europe was often worked in red and white. There is a Lithuanian proverb

ABOVE *A putty-grey bed and tomato-red bedlinen make a sophisticated yet cheerful scheme for a bedroom. Red checks are particularly apt for creating a Scandinavian look.*

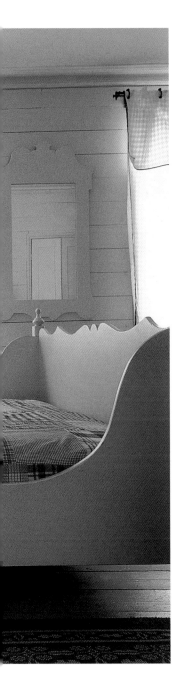

that says: 'What is red is beautiful.' This also holds true to much traditional Swedish decor, fresh and bright. Enamelware washjugs and bowls were once vital accessories for the folk-art bedroom. Again, functional items that were tough and sturdy were made decorative by the application of floral flourishes.

ABOVE *Stencilled walls and handmade floor rugs are folk traditions that never wane in popularity. This modest four-poster bed, with its solid mahogany posts, is made to look less austere by means of pale walls and delicate detailing.*

bed dressing

> *Sleeping is no mean art:*
> *for its sake one must stay*
> *awake all day.*
>
> FRIEDRICH NIETZSCHE
> 1844–1900

In Russia, specially embroidered towels and textiles were made by women as wedding gifts, as Amish quilts often were. They were draped from the ceiling beams of modest peasant wooden houses as both decoration and social statement. In Poland, another wedding tradition was for the women to make pillowcases for pillows that were stuffed with goose down and piled, six or seven high, at the foot of the bed. They were valued because of the intricate embroidery involved, and because the down came from the breast of the goose and was scarce – a far cry from items on today's department-store wedding list.

Children's cot blankets were created in much the same spirit as wedding pillows and quilts, but were also functional, warm pieces of bedlinen. Despite being lovingly handcrafted, these artefacts were not hung on a wall, to be revered as pieces of art: they were in everyday use and often passed on to subsequent generations. Elaborate cross-stitch samplers were often made for bedrooms. Slovakia, the Shaker communities in America and England were all areas in which the creation of samplers flourished. These small canvases bore people's names and key events in their lives such as births, marriages and also new homes.

As industrial processes soon replaced handcrafted decoration, folk art almost died out, but today many traditions have been revived, and surviving antique furniture and textiles are much in demand at auction houses. Craft traditions such as embroidery, blanketwork and also

LEFT *Wool blankets and handstitched eiderdowns always introduce a certain style to bedrooms. The folk aesthetic is closely linked with the fascinating history of quilts.*

RIGHT *The traditional American bed quilt was often produced by a dedicated team of friends and relations, as a wedding gift for a woman to enjoy and pass on to the next generation.*

quiltmaking are again celebrated for their inventiveness and attention to detail rather than dismissed as time-consuming hobbies. The bedroom is one place where such delicate artwork can be fully enjoyed, in the form of embroidered bedlinen, patchwork quilts, handstitched wall hangings and felt blankets edged in blanket stitch.

Traditional rag rugs on the floor, handstitched panels for curtains, even blinds edged in ginghams and quilts made from scraps of your children's favourite outgrown clothes all add to the folk appeal of a bedroom, sustaining the circle of life and encouraging a sense of family history and continuity to prevail.

LEFT *The Dutch Pennysylvanian folk tradition used stylized floral motifs for decoration. Tulips and floral bowers were often painted on to iron bedsteads to great effect.*

RIGHT *Painted bedheads were sometimes the only form of decoration in a peasant bedroom. Artisans travelled from place to place with a set of paints to embellish basic furniture.*

painted tradition

The tradition of decorative painting is still hugely popular in many parts of the world, despite being less prevalent than it once was. During the nineteenth century in Europe, industrial processes and population migration threatened to destroy the vernacular legacies of skill-based design and decoration that had been handed down from one generation to the next. The peasant tradition of decorating domestic furniture and walls produced bright and inviting interiors. Paint was used to cheer up modest rooms rather than to adorn exquisitely made pieces of grand furniture. It was only once the Industrial Revolution had begun, in the 1800s, that many architects and designers became anxious to preserve the vernacular crafts of peasant communities, which had until then always decorated for themselves. Decorative painting encouraged creativity while disguising less than perfect pieces of furniture, producing in the process an individual object for the home, however modest. It is a form of self-expression that has resisted being reduced to an industrial process.

Northern European painted designs tended to use strong but muted shades of china red and apple green, favourites of the Swedish designer Carl Larsson at his celebrated country home Lilla Hyttnäs. Elsewhere, in the Netherlands, France and Germany, milky shades of yellow, blue and grey were popular. Often indigenous materials gave rise to distinctive styles. The Aborigines in Australia and

Space and light and order. These are the things men need just as much as they need bread or a place to sleep.

LE CORBUSIER, 1887–1965

the Ndebele people of Southern Africa create a rainbow of earth shades, using paint made from naturally occurring pigments. In Mexico and the Caribbean, where constant sunshine inspires a vivid palette, bright sherbet pinks and aquas form the basis of colour schemes.

Painting beds and adding naturalistic motifs, such as flowers and leaves, is a decorative practice found everywhere from Europe to Appalachia. Intricately painted red and white designs were applied to cabin beds in Russia Romania and Hungary, while in the Netherlands strong tulip motifs were used. Shaker communities in the United States were entirely preoccupied with simplicity and utility, so their painting was always without embellishment. Their self-constructed beds were not only plain, but were all painted in the same colour, according to their self-imposed Millenial Laws of 1845: 'Bedsteads should be painted green – comfortables (blankets) should be of a modest colour. Blankets for outside spreads should be blue and white, but not checked or striped.'

Today, there are so many colours, fabrics and bed designs to choose from that it is easy to understand the appeal of such rigorous guidelines. Sometimes simplicity is the easiest, as well as the most appealing, option. However, painting beds and bedroom furniture is still a relatively easy way of transforming tired or ordinary pieces of furniture and imposing a cohesive decorative scheme on a bedroom. Linking the furniture colour to that of the soft furnishings can provide a loose colour coordination that if it is not too strictly applied, results in a sense of pleasing harmony.

RIGHT *Shaker beds were plain and simple, in keeping with their philosophy of 'hands to work, hearts to God'. This pleasing shade of deep turquoise blue was frequently used on furniture and woodwork.*

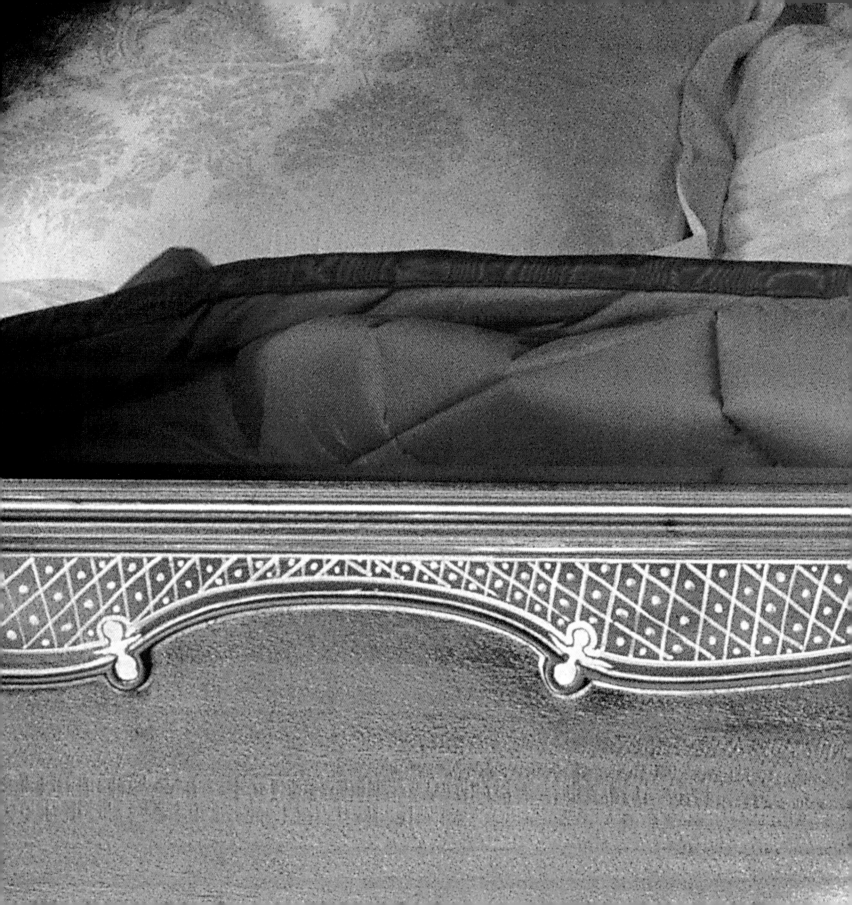

EASTERN exotic

ABOVE *Colourwashed pigment walls and full-length shutters bring the outside into a vivid Mexican bedroom.*

RIGHT *A cool white tiled interior incorporates plinths and banquettes, which form day beds and seating under a canopy of wood and bamboo.*

The best of Eastern exotic style combines ethnic with modern, traditional with minimal, and strong colour with sympathetic materials that epitomize a cheerful, creative and comfortable approach to bedroom living. It takes its inspiration from many periods of history and global sources, from the Far East and the Indian subcontinent, North Africa and the Mediterranean to Mexico and the Caribbean. This global mix encompasses decorative traditions closely connected to climate, indigenous materials and local colours, a result of centuries of trade winds. The British Raj in India introduced a smart colonial imperative to hilltop towns, French colonization in Northern Africa led to a European obsession with Morocco, and the Dutch exploration of Indonesia discovered such natural materials as cane, bamboo and seagrass. Elsewhere, China provided the opulent decorative tradition of chinoiserie.

Exotic bedrooms can be contemporary as well as classic. Christian Liaigre, the celebrated French interior designer who works with natural materials such as jute and hessian, has designed a simple, pared-down retreat on the Indonesian island of Bali that is a perfect mesh of local materials and minimal chic. From South Africa, designer Stephen Falcke has produced award-winning hotel work, creating a new colonial style by combining indigenous craftworks such as carved calabashes and iroko sculptures with bedroom furniture for a smart monochromatic statement with tribal influences. Strong colour combined with simple, interesting bed shapes is the hallmark of bedrooms in lush Moroccan villas, Mexican haciendas and Caribbean seashore homes.

Chinoiserie and its successor, japonaiserie have slid in and out of fashion. Chinoiserie first found favour after the opening up of the silk route in the seventeenth century. People in the West were astonished by the beauty of silks, intricate detailing on furniture, fans, lacquerwork screens and bamboo artefacts. Imitation Oriental lacquerware was developed for wall panelling and bedroom storage, and was referred to as japanning to differentiate it from the authentic work indigenous to the East. The same decorative treatment was applied to bedheads and free-standing pieces such as screens and cupboards.

So popular was the Oriental look that the new industrial processes meant many goods were mass produced in Europe to feed the growing demand. As a result, the original appeal of exoticism and exclusivity began to fade, and the look was not revived until the end of the nineteenth century when Arthur Lasenby Liberty at his adventurous Regent Street store revived imports of the real thing. Suddenly, fashionable Victorian bedrooms were furnished with cane bedside tables, bedsteads of ornate ironwork shaped to emulate bamboo, and cupboards, blanket boxes and wardrobes finely painted with Japanese flower motifs and outdoor scenes. Today, Oriental influences are at play again in the bedroom, but with a contemporary twist. Modern designers such as Kelly Hoppen and Mimi O'Connell have created a fashion for fusion decorating that embraces an 'East Meets West' style, using lacquerwork for bedheads, exotic fabrics for bed dressing and simple graphic shapes for beds, tables and seating made from exotic woods.

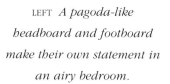

LEFT *A pagoda-like headboard and footboard make their own statement in an airy bedroom.*

BELOW *Forged iron struts lashed together with gold-painted strips of bamboo add Far Eastern appeal to this rustic bedhead.*

Exotic bedrooms embrace any number of distinct looks, including ornate, minimal, ethnic, colourful and colonial. Architecture in hot, exotic locations often allows bedrooms to have a sense of connection with the outside, by means of shuttered windows that can be left open, skylights in the ceiling, fold-back doors and fretwork concrete walls that permit light to filter in, creating instant atmosphere. Filtered light is an important element of exotic bedrooms and can be achieved even in cold climates by using coloured glass and metal lanterns from Morocco, Mexico or India, either suspended from the ceiling or used as wall sconces. Candles placed within lanterns or behind fretwork metal sconces have the same effect, transforming a bedroom into a seductive haven.

Colour and texture are key to a number of exotic-inspired bedrooms. Walls painted in a wash of Mediterranean blue, deep aqua, rich yellow and ochre tones or sherbet shades of pink instantly conjure heat and light. At the other end of the colour spectrum, delicate painted chinoiserie offers a refined vision of the East in which woven cane bedheads and mock-bamboo brass bedheads evoke Oriental elegance.

The charm of exotic influences lies in their simple, often colourful and individual attitude to living. People crave a quiet space in which they can express themselves and recharge in private away from the increasingly frenetic world of mass communication and information. A bedroom decorated in accordance with a distinct cultural identity or in colours that evoke a particular place, is instantly inviting and instinctively pleasurable.

LEFT *A bedroom where the walls and architectural features provide the visual treat needs only an alcove mattress on which to sit and appreciate the fine decoration.*

BELOW *Moroccan lanterns impart instant atmosphere and intimacy in a bedroom.*

exotic beds

An element of fantasy is never far away in an exotic bedroom. Being transported to a favourite overseas destination by means of colour, style of bed or choice of flooring and fabric is at once exciting and relaxing. Exotic beds range from ones with wildly fantastic carved Indian bedheads incorporating ceramic or painted inlays of stylized landscapes to ordinary divans dressed with lush textiles and large cushions to boost their presence; from brightly painted Mexican bedheads in sharp green and tomato red to subtle colonial-style wooden beds with mosquito net drapes and a constantly twirling ceiling fan to prove how hot it is.

Today's contemporary preoccupation with minimal decoration translates well into an exotic bedroom setting. Low-level divans and basic wooden platform beds suit a bohemian ethnic style and can be emboldened with the addition of a strong-coloured luxurious throw. The 1960s conversation pit, with its sunken area filled with ethnic-looking floor cushions, has made a sophisticated comeback in the bedroom, this time with suede, leather and velvet cushions and cubes.

Bed materials, colour, rich fabrics and cool linens are all part of the exotic story, each coming to the fore depending

Yet a little sleep, a little slumber,
a little folding of the hands to sleep.

PROVERBS 6:10

LEFT *A classic wooden bedstead is made more romantic and exotic by the addition of pure white bedlinen and a draped muslin canopy.*

on the ethnic origin of the style, the geographical location and the cultural influence at play. When deciding on an exotic look, it is easy to call up images of special places before deciding on a particular style. Remember, though, that the strength of Caribbean and Mexican colours can sometimes seem too harsh when in the cold light of the Northern hemisphere, whereas earthier and more neutral shades translate well to most countries.

ABOVE *White walls, bedlinen and an upholstered headboard provide a blank canvas that is punctuated by ebony-coloured picture frames, furniture and ethnic objects for a smart African look.*

ABOVE *This wooden bed is decorated with charming bamboo beading and diamonds that hint at Oriental sophistication.*

RIGHT *A sleek-looking lit à la polonaise has been draped with a luscious red silk for an opulent finish.*

The Far Eastern aesthetic combines pale honey-toned canework beds framed with muslin curtains to evoke the clean-lined charm of Indonesia's islands and the rich cultural traditions of Thailand. Natural materials are often used in Far Eastern decoration and there has been a renewed interest in sustainable woods since ecological concerns have become paramount. This has led to a revival of traditional materials for bed design, including cane, bamboo and iroko, used for a variety of furniture such as beds, screens, low-level platforms and bedheads.

The trick in making an exotic scheme work is not to be too strictly authentic. Place a bamboo bed in a modern setting with cool calico and muslin as a backdrop, and you will be swiftly transported to the Far East in spirit, without having to resort to ripping out the carpets or dispensing with a fireplace. Adding wicker tables at the bedside and simple metal lanterns will give an informal, airy look. Canework is enjoying a long-overdue revival and has become a fashionable decorative statement rather than an embarrassing faux pas, and it works equally well in a minimal or an opulent setting.

Bedrooms inspired by the Indian subcontinent are full of decorative fabric and rich in detail. Highly intricate carved mahogany bedsteads from Rajasthan are often draped in sensuous, lush silks in vivid rainbow colours. Other textiles, such as organza, muslin and cotton, are embellished with tiny mirrors and intricate hand embroidery, having just been dyed in gorgeous saturated tones of fuchsia, burnt orange and ruby red, a lavish mix of colour that provides joyful definition.

BELOW *Japanese low-level living allows for a clutter-free, geometrically ruled space where a simple mattress matches the style's understatement.*

Playing with colour in an exotically inspired bedroom calls for an honest appraisal of which colours you and your partner can live and sleep with. One person's cool, calming aquamarine is another's worst nightmare. Strong colour can work in a bedroom, especially if it is applied as a broken wash rather than dense wall panels, but ensure

RIGHT *A faux-bamboo finish on this bed is achieved with paint over a solid iron base.*

*The morning is wiser
than the evening.*

RUSSIAN PROVERB

that both parties agree before covering white walls with burnt orange or berry-red paint. Sometimes painting the bed itself will inject strong colour into a bedroom without the need to decorate the whole room. Accent colour can be provided in the form of cushions, fabric panels on cupboard doors and window treatments.

Buying or adapting an exotic bed is often enough to stamp a particular ethnic or fantasy mark on the room. Forged-metal beds in fantasy designs such as faux bamboo or cowboy leather straps prove popular for those with adventurous ideas about bedroom design. If a higher degree of sophistication is called for, iron and brass bedsteads forged into pagoda-style frameworks give an instant air of the East. Dress them with lustrous, thick eiderdowns or plain silk quilts for a luxurious finish. Keeping the bed and the bedroom furniture simple will also help to elevate the scheme. Use rich textures of walnut, cherry and canework to complement the colour.

Creating a Far Eastern sensibility in the bedroom is a matter of paring down the furnishings, introducing some pale or dark-stained wood and allowing the bed to become a simple symbol of relaxation. Bedheads with inset panels of seagrass, bamboo, cane or calico hint at the exotic climates of the Far East; while making a four-poster with bamboo, thin forged-iron or simple beech poles, laced with muslin panels or canework blinds, is an instant way of framing a plain divan and transporting it a couple of continents away in spirit.

Graphic shapes such as simple wooden cubes for bedside tables, chunky bamboo blocks as headboards and

long-legged cane tables for the foot of the bed give a
bedroom a colonial edge. A colourful and slightly kitsch
Chinese style may be created using paper Chinese lanterns
overhead and by the bed, together with a traditional
Chinese silk bedspread and a simple metal or chrome-
framed bed. Silk scarves used as bed hangings above the
bed, and duvets or bedlinen with thick black Chinese
lettering reinforce the look.

Mediterranean style is often best achieved by combining
blue and white in the bedroom. Walls painted white can be
made to look more Mediterranean by roughing up the
surface to emulate painted brick walls and using strong
deep blue fabrics on the bed. In an East-facing bedroom,
shutters at the windows will let light flood in during the
early morning. Mediterranean beds are often painted
white or blue for a cool breeziness, or left plain but clad in
seaside colours. Striped rugs and runners on wooden or
ceramic floors and simple window treatments evoke
seaside villas, as do simple wrought-iron bedsteads.
Furnishings and furniture tend to be kept to a minimum.

Day beds are often associated with an exotic look.
Outdoor living in warm climates means siestas and even
overnight sleeping outdoors. Mattresses incorporated into
concrete banquettes are often found in Greek seaside
homes or in Moroccan courtyards, beside small water
features that are carefully lit on all sides by punched metal
lanterns and wall sconces. Large cushions provide additional comfort. On verandas, balconies and roof terraces,
some form of fabric canopy is usually put up to provide
shade and decoration.

ABOVE *This tented bed is covered with
muslin suspended from brass rings
that are pushed into the low reed roof,
to create an enclosed retreat where
ethnic fabrics are used on the bed and
the headboard.*

I believe that everything in one's house should be comfortable, but one's bedroom must be more than comfortable: it must be intimate.

ELSIE DE WOLFE, 1870–1950

RIGHT *Red lacquerwork furniture and a gracefully poportioned bed are set off well with white bedlinen and deep plum walls.*

exotic bed textiles

Dressing a bed with rich, sumptuous fabrics in a variety of textures and tones can evoke a variety of places and moods. Hot or warm colours such as saffron, cinnamon, mulberry, mustard and deep fuchsia create a palette that suggests the vivid hues of India. For sheer saturated colour, there is nothing better than a Mexican mix of strong tomato red and apple green or the rich watery tones of aqua teamed with hot pink. Applying these colours, in a generous mix of tones, will always warm up a bed or bedroom and evoke a specific place. Using a particular collection of colours in an interesting combination of tactile velvets, silks, organzas and densely embroidered cottons will create an air of hot charm and opulent luxury, even in the simplest of settings.

Sensuous fabrics work well on bed pillows and cushions that are both decorative and functional. Make up a bed then arrange on it a variety of different-shaped pillows covered in assorted textures, from heavily brocaded or embroidered bolsters with large, ornamental tassels at either end, to plump, square, velvet cushions, plain or trimmed with fringing. A rich mix of colours and shapes is always pleasing to the eye. Alternatively, a combination of plain colours in the form of a satin eiderdown or bedcover, silk cushions or sheets set against rich brocade or even velvet curtains, cannot fail to provide an air of smart but luxurious sensuousness.

LEFT *Shimmering gold satin, burnt-orange silk and deep raspberry bedding: a lush collection of fabrics for an intricate brass bedstead that alludes to the East.*

RIGHT *All the colours of India merge happily on an iron bedstead placed outdoors as a day bed.*

BELOW *Bedlinen can create colourful contrasts against painted bedheads.*

ABOVE *A mixture of stripes, paisley designs and animal prints adds a plush bohemian element to this iron bedstead.*

Tufted Turkish rugs, kelims and bright runners add further fabric interest to an exotic scheme, while softening floorboards, flagstones and tiles. Wall hangings are a way of providing decoration above a simple divan. Sometimes ornate rugs are used for this purpose, but a delicate hand-embroidered Chinese silk panel or handstitched shawl would work well too. Handembroidered Indian crewel-work lends an ethnic air.

Simple bedheads can be embellished and made to coordinate or contrast with fabric decoration elsewhere in the bedroom by simply draping panels of vivid silk over the headboard and stitching on ribbon ties for a smart look.

RIGHT *A red silk throw with pale gold designs woven into it adds a sleek touch to a fine metal bed.*

FAR RIGHT *An Oriental half-tester defined in gold and draped with orange silk includes a gilt mirror, in a pleasing marriage of traditional forms and ethnic style.*

No exotic bedroom would be complete without a mosquito net over the bed or light, filmy fabric at the windows. In India, textiles are used all over the home to lend comfort and colour. In the bedroom, they appear as room dividers, wardrobe fronts and, most commonly, as bed drapes. To provide an enclosing, romantic setting, bed curtains can be made from muslin or sari fabric, either plain or edged with bands of velvet or mirrorwork cotton. Loosely tied with ribbon sashes, rope cord or bands of embroidered mirrorwork, they focus attention on the bed, adding a decorative element in their own right and colour to one of the most important rooms in the home.

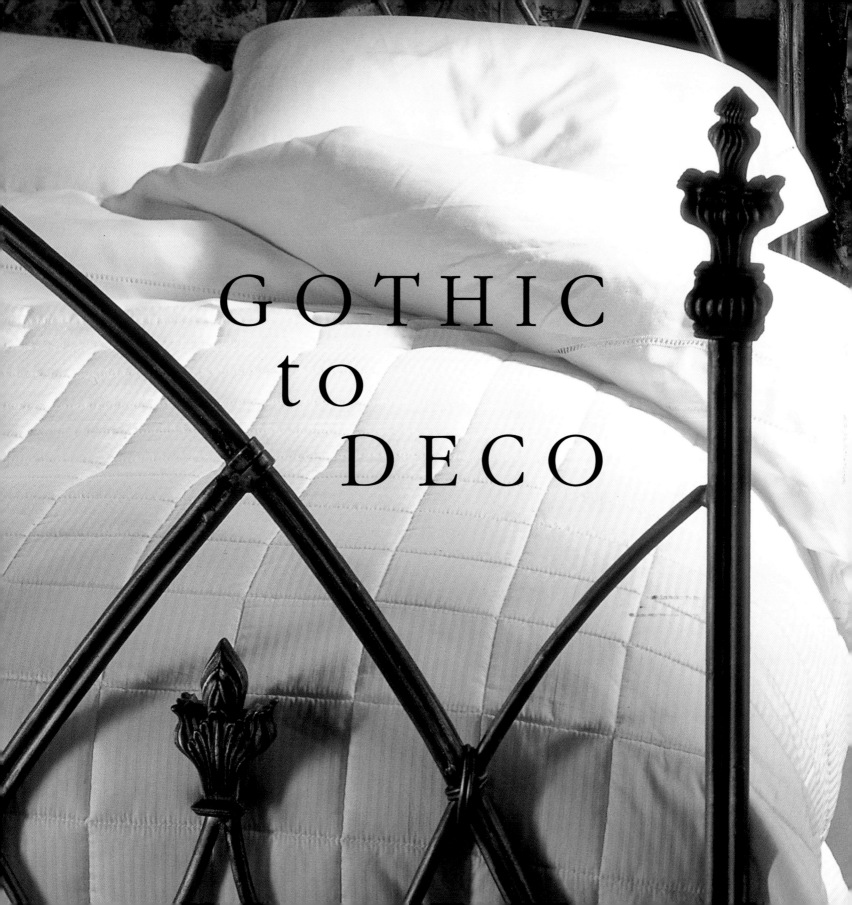

GOTHIC
to
DECO

My candle burns at both ends;
It will not last the night;
But, ah, my foes,
and oh, my friends
It gives a lovely light.

'FIGS FROM THISTLES',
EDNA ST VINCENT MILLAY
1892–1950

The styles of Gothic, Arts and Crafts, Art Deco and Art Nouveau each have a distinct look that is highly stylized, unmistakable and enduring. Each continues to be held in affection by a substantial number of home decorators, fascinated by the materials, colours and forms that sum up a particular period and ethos. Beds of each period, some championed and designed by individual architects and designers, are instantly recognizable today, and classic designs reproduced for devotees of the styles. A.W. Pugin was an architect who pioneered the Gothic Revival during the early and mid-1800s. William Morris pioneered the Arts and Crafts Movement from the 1850s on. The designs of Serge Diaghilev's Ballets Russes in the early 1920s signified an influential shift from Art Nouveau to Art Deco, which evolved from the Paris Exposition Internationale in 1925 to become high Art Deco in France and the beginnings of a 'Moderne' movement elsewhere in Europe. The Scottish architect Charles Rennie Mackintosh's white bedroom was groundbreaking, daring and innovative. His name is synonymous with Art Nouveau and the beginnings of Modernism.

Each of these periods has specific decorative elements that conjure up the era. Features such as chrome Deco bedroom lights, Gothic-arched bed frames or Arts and Crafts wood-panelled beds and furniture may stand alone as decorative testaments to a particular style, or can be used together, to form a complete look.

Gothic style arose in the middle of the nineteenth century as a richly detailed approach to decoration that had its roots in the medieval period. The Houses of

RIGHT *Medieval Gothic beds were shrouded with bed curtains and fitted with solid, chunky wooden headboards and footboards to preserve warmth in rooms where stone walls and draughts conspired against them.*

Parliament in London are a fine example of this style, which relied on ecclesiastical references for much of its exterior and interior decoration. Gables, coloured brickwork and Gothic arched windows on the outside, rich deep red, blue and green embossed wallpapers within, emboldened with repeating fleur-de-lys motifs, are an enduring memorial to the architect, Pugin.

Recreating Gothic style in the bedroom inevitably calls for some form of elongated arches. These can be part of a carved wooden or wrought-iron bedhead, appear on a rich oak screen that divides the room, or serve as window shutters. In original Gothic bedrooms, arched detailing was in the form of plaster cornicework, as painted decoration traced on to walls or woodwork and wooden panelling around a room. Signature Gothic colours are deep midnight blue, rich moss green and muddy pink terracotta. Star motifs also add to the atmosphere. Neo-Gothic influences gave rise to iron beds with Gothic arched bedheads and small posts bearing brass and iron plumed feather motifs which are much reproduced today. These are popular designs since they work well in both country and urban settings, their simplicity a good foil for a number of decorative styles.

Arts and Crafts displays sympathy for the natural 'honest' virtues and smooth surfaces of wood, and a preoccupation with the relationship between beauty and function. The Movement was in part a reaction against the Industrial Revolution's mass-production techniques and sparked a revival of interest in handcrafted design using natural materials of quality and integrity.

ABOVE *A Gothic-inspired forged iron bedstead is softened and made welcoming with the addition of crisp white sheets and an attractive beige bedspread.*

LEFT *This Gothic four-poster combines elegance with period detailing to create a loose but appealing reference to more formal predecessors.*

Chunky, solid wooden beds dressed with natural fabrics, sturdy post-beds in panelled bedrooms and polished steel bedheads with satin eiderdowns mark the stylistic changes that began during the 1850s with William Morris and his decorating company. Arts and Crafts is a look of honesty and integrity, function and beauty that has remained constantly in fashion, reflecting the universal relevance of furniture that is both useful and beautiful.

LEFT *Intricate marquetry adds floral decoration to a streamlined walnut and beech Art Deco bedhead.*

RIGHT *A forged pewter bedhead incorporating Gothic arches and detailing such as this would echo the ecclesiastical references of a church conversion.*

Art Deco, which began during the 1920s was an altogether more chic and glamorous decorative style in which beds became more sensuous and exotic. Brushed-steel bedheads in Odeon shapes of interlocking geometric motifs were perfectly set off by satin eiderdowns and bedspreads. Mint julep, raspberry crush, shimmery gold and sparkly silver were the colours of the period, each reflective and translucent in tone. Bedroom furniture of this time was solid and curvy, with walnut and oak the favoured woods. Dressing tables and bedside tables were all designed in a sympathetic Odeon style that matched bedsteads, and the overall look was one of solid elegance. The interiors of classic ships such as the *Queen Mary*, now preserved as a hotel in Long Beach, California, have room after room panelled in wood heavy with the Deco feel.

Deco-style beds in polished steel are collectors' items these days but reproductions are plentiful. Chrome and polished steel suit many contemporary rooms, while adding a retro note to a modern urban space. A retro bed is a comfortable and sumptuous addition to a bedroom, suggesting nights of pampered slumber.

arts and crafts

LEFT *William Morris adapted the bed he was born in at Walthamstow, London, for his home at Kelmscott Manor and added bed curtains and wallpaper in one of his most famous designs.*

RIGHT *This wooden panelled bed has an Arts and Crafts sensibility and an oak finish in keeping with the period.*

The Arts and Crafts Movement of the nineteenth century was emblematic of a new approach to interior design that involved a fresh, naturalistic approach to materials. It flourished on both sides of the Atlantic, from the elegant neo-Gothic beauty of William Morris's Red House in Kent, England to the wood interiors of the Greene brothers' houses in Pasadena, California. The movement marked a transition from the machine aesthetic to an approach that was more in sympathy with nature, simplicity and artistry. Taking the florid ornament of Gothic style and shaping it to create harmonious, integrated interiors that included fabric and tapestries, embroidery and decorative painting, Morris inspired a whole new generation of craftspeople and architects such as Charles Rennie Mackintosh, C.F.A. Voysey and Sir Edwin Lutyens to create rooms of a particularly enduring appeal.

Beds became integrated into complete bedroom schemes where the wood panelling on the walls echoed that used for beds and their complementary furniture. Function and decoration combined to produce bedheads of solid oak, chiselled to include stylized images of birds, fruit and other images from nature. Wallpaper was very much to the fore, with Morris's naturalistic designs in great demand. They remain hugely popular today and continue to be mass-produced by Sanderson & Co, not just in the form of wallpaper, but also by Liberty as furnishing fabrics, notebooks, plastic-coated tablecloths, bags, umbrellas and any other item you care to imagine.

Mackintosh and art nouveau

The Arts and Crafts-inspired sensibility of Charles Rennie Mackintosh, the Scottish architect and designer, has remained remarkably fresh and appealing. There is a thriving industry devoted to reproducing Mackintosh 'memorabilia' in the form of earrings, silk scarves and drinks coasters that bear his distinctive geometric and stylized designs.

LEFT AND BELOW *Taking the work of Scottish architect and designer Charles Rennie Mackintosh as a starting point, this oak fretwork headboard and black lacquered bed are tributes to his distinctive approach to interior design.*

RIGHT *An original Mackintosh bedroom at Hill House in Scotland displays his hallmark geometric styling.*

Today, Mackintosh's work is much appreciated for the cool, calm and innovative interiors he designed for Hill House in Helensburgh, Scotland and his own apartment home in Glasgow. This universal appeal has obvious parallels with the way in which Carl Larsson's simple Swedish home became an icon of accessible style, reproduced on cookie tins and posters throughout 1970s Sweden. Although the images became diluted through commercialism and familiarity, the design message has remained intact. Mackintosh's apartment home is now a museum that still impresses and inspires bed and bedroom designers; its white painted beds and integral storage, simple bed curtains in pale hues of white and grey decorated with his wife's designs, and bespoke matching furniture adorned with Glasgow roses reproduced in an Art Nouveau-like form, are unmistakably representative of his unique approach to interiors.

Mackintosh's signature achromatic palette of whites, greys and blacks was used at Hill House to great effect, and he later went on to design oak and black lacquered furniture making further use of his grid designs. His awareness of Oriental finishes such as lacquerwork inspired him to design black lacquered beds that still look remarkably contemporary.

Gridded headboards have an innate simplicity that is modern, graphic and versatile, and lend themselves to contemporary interiors that take a sparse approach to furniture and furnishings. Quite masculine in appearance, this type of bed looks best in an uncluttered environment where colour schemes are restrained.

deco style

Art Deco was primarily a decorative arts movement, but its groundbreaking use of new materials, motifs and form inevitably went on to influence architecture and interiors. It began in France at the beginning of the twentieth century, where new materials from the French colonies were used to create lush one-off pieces of furniture of the highest quality and craftsmanship. Unfamiliar exotic elements such as macassar ebony, mother-of-pearl, ivory, tortoiseshell, amboyna wood, burr walnut and palmwood were used to embellish bedheads, dressing tables, cabinets, screens and chaises longues. Surfaces were rarely left plain, and dressing tables were likely to be finished with leather or parchment panelling, with silk tassels as drawer pulls. Rich veneers were applied to bedheads in the form of ivory, tortoiseshell and horn.

Such scarce materials are no longer legally exploitable so today's versions of these bedroom pieces evoke the style in shape, look and form rather than materials, although leather, veneers, lacquerwork and tubular chromework are enough to recreate the style.

The 1920s and 1930s, sandwiched between two world wars, constituted a period of great change in interior decoration. The further development of the machine aesthetic opened up new possibilities in metalwork. A worldwide Depression was counterpointed by a return to glamour and fantasy, fuelled by the machine age and the availability of exciting new materials such as bronzework and chrome.

LEFT *An Odeon-style upholstered bed has a soft, tactile suede-like headboard and footboard that are finished off with chunky chrome feet for an elegant and streamlined bedroom.*

To counteract the global Depression, interior design fostered a mood of glamour and seduction that coincided with Hollywood entering its golden period of talkies and large film studios investing in building high-style Art Deco-inspired movie houses. Hotels followed the lush extravagance of the new look, providing exquisite rooms, especially on Miami Beach in Florida.

Bedroom design reflected the fantasy images served up by the sumptuous, big-production values of the time, embodied by Busby Berkeley movies and Hollywood idols such as Rita Hayworth, Gary Cooper and Jean Harlow. Bedrooms became palaces of sensuality, with large layered mirrors, new oval and round bed shapes, and bedheads with geometric chevrons, sunbursts, animal motifs and stylized flowers. Odeon-style headboards were covered in buttoned satin for sheer seduction; shiny chrome feet were applied to divan beds; and reflective surfaces such as coloured glass panels, bronze and silver panelling,

lacquerwork and chrome metal were used on everything from bed frames and chests of drawers to free-standing screens, windows and doors. Wooden bed frames in exotic woods such as walnut were also popular.

Bedroom fabrics, too, were influenced by animal motifs. Throws and bedspreads appeared in leopardskin prints, black and white ponyskin and zebra stripes. Art Deco also influenced a new wave of Moderne designers and architects including Le Corbusier. His Grand Confort 1928 day bed, covered in ponyskin, successfully combines supreme quality with high design.

Today, hints of Art Deco abound in contemporary bedrooms created by exciting new interior designers such as Jonathan Reed in London and Stephen Falcke in South Africa. Fake fur throws, chrome 1930s-style wall lights, veneered and leather headboards, velour upholstery, silk bedding and lacquerwork bedroom furniture are all re-emerging and being used judiciously in modern settings.

LEFT *Curvy furniture, animal prints and a preoccupation with gold, silver, bronze and chrome are all indicative of the Art Deco style of decoration.*

LEFT *Chrome metal beds were characteristic of the austerity years and are once again popular in bedrooms with an ascetic edge.*

CONTEMPORARY
classics

ABOVE *This 'Tree of Life' bed has a sinuous presence that animates the space of a grand bedroom.*

RIGHT *A platformed area of this bedroom houses two symmetrical divans dressed in pink and finished with yellow cushions. Graphic shapes and bold blocks of colour make this Mexican bedroom startlingly simple and beautifully low key.*

Today's preoccupations with contemporary design and a pared-down approach to the home have obviously had a significant impact on bedrooms. Yet many traditional bed designs can look strikingly modern in the right setting, their basic contours suited to the obsession with clean lines, low maintenance and economic decoration associated with the urban minimal aesthetic.

People are often surprised to find that Modernism is nearly a century old and that today's spare, contemporary interiors sometimes revisit the style of the machine age and the early Modernist architects and designers such as Le Corbusier and Mies van der Rohe, but with a new twist on their maxims of function and simplicity. Homes where technology has replaced artifice, and decoration relies on colour and texture more than pattern, have dispensed with the cosy period bedroom look in favour of a cool and calm sleeping space.

The two key elements of the contemporary bedroom are a bed that offers comfort and an understated elegance. Simple forms such as low-level platforms in beech epitomize the style, as do clean-lined built-in clothes storage and the modern mantra of space and light to provide a backdrop for furnishings that are natural in inspiration.

Converted spaces such as lofts, disused churches, former factories and barns often contain the most successful contemporary bedrooms. These large spaces in old buildings are often those that manage to merge details of the old and new in a curiously fruitful symbiosis. When a cutting-edge bed is the focal piece of furniture in a modern space,

it is undoubtedly enhanced by the addition of an older detail, such as an antique mirror or a battered period chest of drawers. A discreet mix of eclectic and new often produces a feeling of soft modern luxury that is impossible to dissect when all the elements are working well in harmony together.

Decorating such a space is a matter of concentrating on materials as much as furniture and form. Wooden blinds, roller blinds and roman blinds all work well in bedrooms where function is key. Wooden flooring or natural matting are sympathetic solutions in a space where dust should be discouraged. Adding softness in the form of sheepskin rugs, striped runners or thick-pile rugs is a flexible way of shifting colours and decoration seasonally. Since a bed is such an investment, contemporary decoration allows a great deal of flexibility when compared with other styles. By swapping round throws, rugs and bedlinen in a neutral space, you can inject colour, change textures and create atmosphere far more easily than in a more scrupulously

LEFT Slipped neatly between the white rafters of a loft conversion is an arched black bed frame that playfully challenges the straight lines elsewhere in the room.

coordinated period scheme. Blinds and fabric panels are more economical to mix and match too.

Natural sleep soothers in contemporary bedrooms include fragrance sticks, scented candles and the feng-shui recommendation of running water (although the effect this might have on nocturnal bladder control needs to be borne in mind). Adjustable light levels are important in spaces that are more empty than most, as is a sense of nature provided in the form of plants, a wind chime and a window that opens wide.

ABOVE Lighting is especially important in contemporary bedrooms where strict simplicity can sometimes be too austere. A cylindrical cane bedside light here casts pleasing watery shadows over the walls for a relaxed atmosphere.

contemporary beds

Contemporary decorating is often considered to be a purely urban preoccupation, but a modern approach to decoration and design can work just as well in a country barn conversion or period home as long as the proportions of the space are sensitively handled. Sometimes a totally modern atmosphere arises from an amalgamation of old and new elements. A nostalgic and timeworn floral eiderdown may be tucked over a tubular-steel frame; a fake fur throw lends warmth and comfort to a simple mattress on top of a low-level retro divan.

Painting a bedroom in shades of taupe, biscuit and stone will provide a calm, neutral backdrop, but a modern mood can be created even if the bed is a period piece or reinterpretation of a traditional classic. Le Corbusier's 1920s chaise longue still appears refreshingly modern, and the sinuous form of a polished mahogany Biedermeier becomes a dignified presence in a contemporary setting. The design may date from the 1800s, but set in a white loft, its elegance speaks for itself. The traditional shape and detailing may have been slightly adapted, but the basic form remains relevant in a contemporary interior.

Wooden beds often work extremely well in modern settings. Pale beech, ash and maple all look good because they blend in with natural colours and textures. Dark woods, too, such as walnut, mahogany and oak, strike a pleasing contrast in bright, light spaces.

LEFT *Thin bed bases slotted between two walls, cabin-style, make the simplest of bunk beds and create an ordered elegance in a small space.*

RIGHT *An iron bed with naturalistic detailing is a delicate, modern version of the traditional ·posted bed that works in a variety of settings.*

Some modern conveniences such as sofa beds and trundles are surprisingly old. Early sofa bed bed mechanisms have been found in Germany dating from around 1833, though they became more common after 1840. Trundles were used in grand country houses for servants to sleep on long before loft living became fashionable and fold away beds were considered chic accessories for studio dwellers.

The amount of sleep required by the average person is just five minutes more.

ANON

LEFT *A sleek, ultra-modern day bed is perfectly suited to this traditional period interior, which has been painted white to create a feeling of open space. A polished wooden floor lightens the room and means natural textures prevail.*

RIGHT *This birch headboard has a maple veneer and punched holes for a supremely modern look. Much contemporary furniture is designed to give flexibility, and this headboard is easily swapped for a different style when the mood takes you.*

Day beds are integral to a contemporary interior and are often placed in a living room or hallway, as well as replacing the traditional chaise longue at the foot of or near a conventional bed. Neither a sofa nor a bed, the day bed can be used as both, a flexible piece of furniture that reflects the contemporary notion of versatility and utility. The starkest versions are beech or plywood frames topped with a thin but sturdy mattress. Among the most luxurious are reproductions of Florence Knoll's twentieth-century chic and elegant day bed, consisting of a leather-uphol-stered cushion on a tubular steel frame, topped at one end with a chunky bolster. Even the reproductions are quite expensive and the originals are highly prized.

New versions of the classic day bed have been designed by Matthew Hilton. His S-shaped bed resting within a rectangle of Lloyd Loom canework is an instant classic, alluding to 1930s materials while being scrupulously sleek in its design.

Industrial and institutional design have also found their way into modern bedrooms. Metal-framed, super-sturdy hospital beds on wheels have for a long time been favoured by Post-Modern architects, while simple four-poster bed frames constructed from scaffolding have also been intro-duced, bringing minimal, recycled design to its logical conclusion. Traditional boarding school dormitory beds fit into the ethos too, bringing with them the wooden tuck box for use as a linen chest or informal bedside table.

Alongside the industrial aesthetic, many contemporary bedrooms display an innovative approach to materials. Plywood, MDF (medium density fibreboard), steel and

even Perspex have all been used by new designers such as Matthew Hilton, Spencer Fung and Tom Dixon to create low-level box constructions that house a mattress. Matthew Hilton's Byron Bed is a good example of simple materials and plain styling combining to create an elegant bed frame. It rests on low tapered legs that make the bed only 30cm (12in) off the ground. Also suited to the 'empty space' ethos are the increasingly popular integrated sleeping systems that comprise low-level wooden platforms on over-sized heavy-duty castors, complete with integral headboard, side tables and halogen spotlights.

Perhaps the ultimate in industrial chic is the anti-design approach championed by Tom Dixon in his MDF-bound book tribute to the genre. Using four piles of builders' bricks as plinths and laying a large piece of plywood on top, you need just a sturdy mattress to create a Post-Modern design statement. A more sophisticated urban refinement belongs to Spencer Fung, the London-based architect responsible for the interiors of the Joseph stores. He draws on his cultural links with the Far East in order to soften the pared-down look for an urban audience. His upholstered bedheads, covered in elegant linen, are simultaneously traditional and modern in feel, standing neatly behind a chunky divan dressed in crisp white sheets and a cashmere throw. Using upholstery on the bedhead is a good way of linking the soft furnishings in a contemporary bedroom. Simple slips made up in natural fabrics such as hessian, Egyptian cotton and linen, or tactile, strokable brushed cotton can be slotted on to MDF panels and varied from season to season.

ABOVE *A looped metal headboard and footboard impart fluidity to an otherwise geometric frame.*

BELOW *Platform beds, which are little more than a solid piece of wood attached to low legs, are extremely popular with loft-dwellers and disciples of contemporary style, their clean lines offering an appealing sense of order in an often chaotic world.*

simplicity is the key

BELOW *Horizontal planes of colour make an interesting palette with an oak headboard and white pillows set against lilac and deep blue bedding.*

Japanese design is closely linked to contemporary considerations. Traditional Japanese bedrooms are scrupulously modern in appearance to Western eyes. Tatami mats, made by springy natural materials such as rice straw and reeds, are laid on the bedroom floor to form a soft base for a futon mattress that is simply unrolled at night and hidden behind a screen by day. These screens, *fusuma*, which separate spaces in Japanese homes, are often incorporated into contemporary bedroom design. Usually they are wooden-framed sliding doors that are left natural or painted black; their grid-like design is covered with rice paper, matting or sheer fabric and is often used on freestanding panels as well.

RIGHT *A sense of calm reigns in such an empty yet appealing space. A blossom-filled vase gives a whisper of nature above this scrupulously simple divan bed.*

Modern Oriental bedheads are always simple, often a gridded framework of black or red lacquer. Authentic Oriental lacquerware, with its high sheen surface, was built up with as many as forty layers of paint derived from the sap of the lac tree. Skilled decorative painters of the nineteenth century soon refined techniques that quite closely copied the look. Traditional black and red lacquering is remarkably elegant and luscious, with a glossy patina that is so smart you hardly dare touch it.

Paper lampshades, first designed by Isamu Noguchi in Japan, have survived many fashion shifts to become contemporary design classics. Differing organic shapes and sizes in neutral shades of cream and white make them

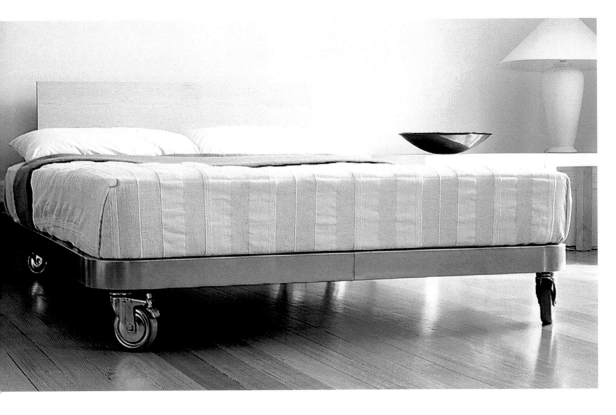

LEFT *Beds on castors are favoured by many of today's architects and designers. The obvious benefits of being able to move a bed around for cleaning or altering a room's layout fit in well with the modern mantra of low maintenance and functionalism.*

RIGHT *The celebrated minimalist John Pawson creates clean spaces in which surfaces are the decoration. Here a beech panel is the only relief in an all-white bedroom.*

a good choice for Japanese, contemporary and ethnic bedrooms. Today they are available as table lamps and on strings, providing novelty and subtlety for the bedside.

One contemporary designer who draws on the Japanese asethetic is Kelly Hoppen, whose signature 'East Meets West' style mixes Oriental simplicity with exoticism for colour and control, while Anouska Hempel has created bedrooms for The Hempel hotel in London that are as near to a shrine-like Zen aesthetic as you can get. The clean lines, crisp sheets and low-level divans are sophisticated symbols of the new calm.

Low-level living has become exceedingly popular with a new generation who are discovering for the first time the happy informality of the beanbag, the easy elegance of low platform beds, the flexibility of simple futons and the sheer economy of mattresses laid directly on to a floor.

What were once hippy prerogatives are now mainstream requisites for a stress-free environment. Joss sticks are reincarnated as fragrance sticks and the art of sleep is a spiritual rejuvenation, along the lines of Zen-inspired living. Who can blame a generation that works hard, grapples with a technological revolution every bit as significant as the Industrial Revolution, and for whom leisure hours are a curious mix of exercise and shopping, often at the expense of personal renewal? No wonder sleep has become such a pressing preoccupation.

Once the preserve of more traditional Japanese homes, low-level living attracts busy people who long to unwind and recharge in a pared-down, simply furnished space. The Zen philosophy of preserving a calm physical space in order to clear the mind is a furnishing mantra that is particularly pertinent for the bedroom. The principles of feng-shui, the Chinese belief system that improves energy flows for a healthier balance, also come into play.

contemporary bed dressing

The contemporary bedroom in which a simple, large bed is the one statement piece, surrounded by clear floor space and subtle lighting can look like a monk's cell unless there is other visual interest. This is where texture and colour become all-important. Add an extra level of interest by introducing a luscious fake fur throw or a thick waffle blanket. If the walls and bed are neutral insert a sharp jolt of colour in the form of jewel-bright turquoise or red cushions and bolsters. Organic materials such as wool, cotton, hessian and linen are easy companions for a naturally decorated bedroom and tone in well against wooden beds to produce a warm mix of textures.

Crisp white and buttermilk cotton sheets are ultra-compatible with cool, modern bedrooms, reflecting a passion for clear colour and functional simplicity. If the bed is the focal point in the room, coloured sheets and a toning bedcover will make a dramatic statement, as will a muslin canopy. Strictly organic bedlinen, such as unbleached cotton sheets, scrunchy linen throws and pillowcases, and sheepskin throws are gentle additions to smart bedrooms, providing a natural link between the minimal and the industrial. For a funky approach to new materials, industrial-inspired inflatable pillows, printed plastic shower curtains or tablecloths radiant with patterns and used as bed drapes will add a strong element of kitsch, with lava lamps an optional extra.

LEFT *Solid, Shaker-style bedside tables make elegant adjuncts to an otherwise plain bed in a room where planes of muted colour and texture benefit from natural light that brings them alive.*

RIGHT *The Hempel hotel in London, is a pure palace of minimalism that is highly popular and scrupulously maintained.*

FAR RIGHT *Cotton piquet bedlinen is perfect for white-on-white bed dressing.*

The four-poster bed appears in even the most modern settings. Scaffolding frameworks, cast iron poles and solid beech posts are all modern interpretations of the traditional form. Contemporary bed hangings include candy-striped banners, feminine organzas and layered muslin in vivid shades. Plain cotton sheeting can be made up into easy tie-or tab-headed drapes that are simple to attach.

GREAT

escapes

The bedroom is the one area in the house that offers an escape from everyday life. And the bed itself is the ultimate escape, a place for romance, refuge and renewal. Creating a pocket of space in which the bed becomes a self-contained haven means that wherever you live and however small the space is, you can climb into bed and be magically transported to a different place.

Sleeping on the move is often a holiday in itself. Canal boats, caravans, cabins on trains and boats, yachts and camper vans all have individual appeal. Their beds are usually compact and built-in, offering a small sanctuary within an enclosed space. In these types of beds a sense of instant warmth is required, so blankets, generously filled sleeping bags and fitted sheets are invaluable. A splash of colour will enliven the area; a spotlight means others need not be disturbed by midnight reading.

Favourite places to escape to can include recreational vehicles and boats where the bed is part of the furniture and fittings. Favourite time-out destinations are the country, sea and mountains, as well as the open road and waterways on which the transport itself provides comfortable sleeping arrangements. Train sleepers, cabin beds on barges, in recreational vehicles and tucked into seagoing sailing boats are all such places. Being gently rocked to sleep while a vehicle propels you to a new destination is an experience that frees you of responsibility and allows the unpredictability of life 'on the road' to liberate you from your usual routine. In such situations sleep is never better, as a constant sense of adventure is a tiring experience, often inducing a deep and restorative slumber.

LEFT *Finding space in a home for a quiet area in which to put your feet up is as good as taking to your bed for a serious nap. The addition of a comforting real fire guarantees relaxation.*

RIGHT *A bolt-hole tucked into the eaves of a country house and screened with heavy drapes fosters dreaming, sleeping and escape.*

The minimalist, Zen-inspired designer Anouska Hempel has created an entire ocean-going yacht in the manner of a cool, colonial interior. Simple divan day beds in neutral stripes are surrounded by bamboo tables, cane roller blinds for instant shade and, of course, the reflective sunshine and sound of water that create infinite permutations for the senses.

Transportable beds that fold away and go with you – among them day beds, campaign or field beds and hammocks – are useful and appealing companions for a nomadic existence. They encourage in us a desire to pack up our bags and disappear for a holiday, a sun-seeking extravaganza or a solitary flight of fancy.

Sleeping under the stars, on the move or at sea is a way of reclaiming our links with nature and recapturing a simplicity of experience often denied us. Children will especially adore the idea of such freedom. A hammock or tent in the garden seems like the ultimate adventure, while a tree house or rowing boat reminds us of nostalgic images from *Swiss Family Robinson* or *Swallows and Amazons*.

People who are lucky enough to own a second home know only too well the sense of escape in retreating to a quiet place for weekends and holidays. Entertaining guests overnight will often call for a flexible approach to sleeping arrangements and beds. Bunk beds, cabins and single beds, as well as sofa beds and chairs, can prove the best solutions for holiday homes where different configurations of guests can be expected. Beds that are light enough to be easily moved from one room to another are also valuable assets to have.

I arise from dreams of thee
In the first sweet sleep of night.
When the winds are breathing low,
And the stars are shining bright.

'THE INDIAN SERENADE'
PERCY BYSSHE SHELLEY, 1792–1822

ABOVE *Furnishing a bedroom*
retreat with artefacts that conjure
favourite places is a good way
of temporarily transporting
yourself elsewhere.

LEFT *In Tigre del Mar, Mexico, a*
jewel-bright ocean is echoed in the
colourwashed walls of this seaside
retreat. A white day bed and table
are sheltered from hot sun to
provide an outdoor haven.

Whether you want to create a comfortable guest room in the country or make an instant bedroom in a tent, there are several key elements to consider. The bed itself may not be the most opulent in the world, but you can boost the comfort factor by placing foam on top of an ageing mattress for extra bulk and using a generously filled duvet and squat, plump pillows for a hint of luxury. Soft sheets and a cool-coloured, textured blanket or throw will create an instant sense of warmth. Make sure there is bedside lighting for reading, and a vase of fresh flowers shows you have truly thought about welcoming your guests. Simplicity is often the best policy for guest bedrooms, as it aids the escape from busy days and cluttered diaries.

Only dull people are brilliant at breakfast.

'AN IDEAL HUSBAND'
OSCAR WILDE, 1854–1900

LEFT A soft, comfortable leather armchair placed near a window, for a quiet moment away from the daily routine, can be substituted by a bed that is similar in feel.

RIGHT A beach retreat on Long Island contains a quiet corner replete with a chunky well-upholstered day bed, reading material and a window view.

great escape beds

LEFT *The epitome of indoor/ outdoor living, this beach house is open to the elements while harbouring a private space at its centre. White and natural colours allow the day beds and chairs to merge into the seascape.*

RIGHT *This richly dressed and well designed four-poster in the Georgian style is an escape in itself, a place for sheer indulgence.*

Beds that offer a sense of escape include enduringly romantic four-posters, high brass beds rich with white crisp cotton bedlinen and inviting throws, and solid wooden bed frames placed enticingly so they dominate the space and look welcoming. The notions of escape and romance are inextricably linked, and the brass bed is often the bed most people think of in this connection. Its familiarity, sense of comfort and country connotations make it an obvious choice, and the wide variety of sizes and styles confer additional flexibility.

Beds in romantic settings are always alluring. Day beds placed on verandas are irresistible, as are campaign beds in safari-like canvas tents. Position beds so you can lie on them and appreciate views over a mountain lake, lush landscapes or urban rooftops, enchancing the sense of escape and detachment from the everyday.

In holiday places, flexible beds that move where you do may not always be the most comfortable to sleep upon, but their versatility makes up for it. Campaign beds, so-called because they were used by the military, are the most obvious temporary guest beds, folding up when not in use. They range from traditional concertina wood-framed examples fitted with a canvas base to a metal-framed version that comes complete with a slim sprung mattress for a greater degree of comfort. Mobile dormitory-style single beds on castors can be moved from room to room,

while metal bunks with a pull-out sofa along the bottom are perfect for small spaces or teenagers. Futons or futon mattresses are useful to keep permanently at hand for extra guests, as are foam squares that fold out to become an instant single bed. Single or double wooden truckle beds with pull-out sections make sense in rooms that need to be shared occasionally.

A permanent supply of extra bedlinen means that impromptu sleepovers or a spontaneous trip to the country are easy to undertake. Store in a blanket box or in drawers under the bed. Bedlinen in plain colours or simple patterns is more versatile than motifs in bold colours.

Creating a space in which to sleep under the stars is a good way of blurring the divide between indoors and outdoors. Large patios with awnings will easily accommodate a hammock on a stand, while built-in concrete banquettes can be furnished with generous cushions for deep comfort. Decking and verandas lend themselves to swinging seats, or simply wheeling out a metal bed and suspending a mosquito net from above on a hot evening. Steamer chairs literally strewn with loose cushions are

ABOVE *A faux-leather bedstead provides a fantasy version of the Wild West that no doubt encourages traveller's tales of the highest order.*

LEFT *Pull-out truckle beds are good sources of extra accommodation for unexpected guests.*

RIGHT *A safari-style bed in the great outdoors recaptures a simple way of living that is innately appealing to everyone from small-space urban dwellers to regular outdoor types.*

comfortable, as are ample hammocks strung up securely between two trees.

Safari-style stone-coloured tents with large flaps make an inviting home from home. Oil lamps suspended from the ceiling, simple campaign beds and, of course, a mosquito net, whether for necessity or decorative effect, will bring the African savannah to any setting.

Mobile homes provide a constant means of escape. Caravans, retro recreational vehicles, trailers and camper vans all thrive on an innovative approach to compact living. Bed spaces become banquettes by day or fold up discreetly into the roof. Floor space is often pressed into service with a mattress laid over it, and long seats convert into sleeping platforms at journey's end.

cabins and retreats

In gardens where there is spare space, create a microcosm of the home or an entirely independent environment by painting and decorating a garden shed, purpose-built log cabin, beach hut, summer house, boat house or tree house. Sleeping in a converted space close to home is an easily achieved means of escape for older children and adults. Roald Dahl famously wrote most of his books in a Romany caravan permanently sited in his garden. Writing into the night, he would often sleep there too.

Even a humble garden shed can be transformed into a log cabin with the help of paint, built-in bunk beds and a curtain at the window. Using sheds and cabins outside the home as additional guest bedrooms is both a practical and a romantic notion.

Tree houses appeal to the child within us, allowing us to create and decorate a sleeping space that is both miniature and different, a peaceful sanctuary that is close to our everyday lives yet away from it all, nestling in a high place with only a rope ladder for access but with privileged views. Children love the escapism and adventure of such a space, while adults appreciate the seclusion and novelty element that a tree-top retreat gives. The best tree houses appear to be organic extensions of natural structures, seamless constructions that are built from logs, strong twisted willow or wooden bargeboarding that sit well in a mature tree.

LEFT *This charming Georgian tree house fits snugly into a grand oak tree and makes an inviting place for sleeping close to nature.*

RIGHT *A Romany caravan is both romantic and functional, allowing life on the road to become a colourful yet practical experience.*

ABOVE *This contemporary
log cabin has bleached
walls and floors, and a
squashy chair and footstool
for extra comfort.
Relaxation comes easy in a
space as enticing as this.*

Boat houses have the soothing presence of water and are
often charming wooden bargeboarded constructions that
lend themselves to a coat of white paint and a simple decorating approach, with ticking mattresses, white bedding
and fishing nets. Small windows can be cosy with checked
curtains. French windows may open out on to riverside
verandas to place hammocks, generous-sized Adirondack
chairs and other sleep-inducing outdoor furniture.

RIGHT *An island home in
Western Australia presents a
colourful interior that jolts
the senses into a feeling of
vitality. A muslin canopy
introduces a hint
of restraint.*

Beach huts and seaside retreats with verandas and views are the perfect escape for those with recollections of happy childhood holidays in small spaces by the sea. The simple sophistication of seaside colours – red, white and blue – makes bedroom decorating easy. Nautical motifs, fabric bunting and flotsam and jetsam are typical components of the look. Natural and nautical elements such as driftwood headboards, large pebbles as doorstops, anchors on walls, striped bedlinen and distressed-wood beds are all quirky, attractive and pleasingly apposite.

Converted barns make idyllic retreats. American barns in soothing paint colours such as barn red and Prussian blue are suitably secluded and punctuate the landscape with warm tones and natural materials. Simply furnished in Shaker or Amish style with wooden beds, handmade quilts and a wood-burning stove, they give all the comfort you need. Brick barns with wooden beams have cavernous space, great views from enlarged windows and a sense of nature close to hand. These converted buildings often feature galleried landings that are ideal for sleeping.

bed and board

Choosing a new mattress is an important decision and one that should not be taken lightly. You (and your partner) need to go into a reputable bed shop and actually lie down and try the various models available. Most furniture showrooms have mattress departments, but you are likely to get better advice from companies that specialize in beds.

Many companies sell beds purely on price and tempt you with extended credit facilities and same-day delivery service. It is simply too easy to disguise an inferior product with good-looking fabrics and a quick and attractive purchase plan. Unfortunately most mattresses look the same, so take the time to find out the differences between inexpensive budget models and the more luxurious styles, which initially may seem to be too extravagant.

The old adage 'you get what you pay for' is applicable to mattress selection. Ultimately your budget will dictate what you order, but ensure that you make an informed choice before making a purchase. Quality of sleep is more important than quantity, and a mattress system that supports correctly is imperative to achieving this. A mattress that is too hard or too soft will guarantee years of disturbed nights tossing and turning, resulting in much irritability, poor health and constant backache.

ABOVE AND LEFT *Mattresses should always be tested before purchasing. Both partners should lie together on a double mattress to gauge how comfortable they both are before any decision is made.*

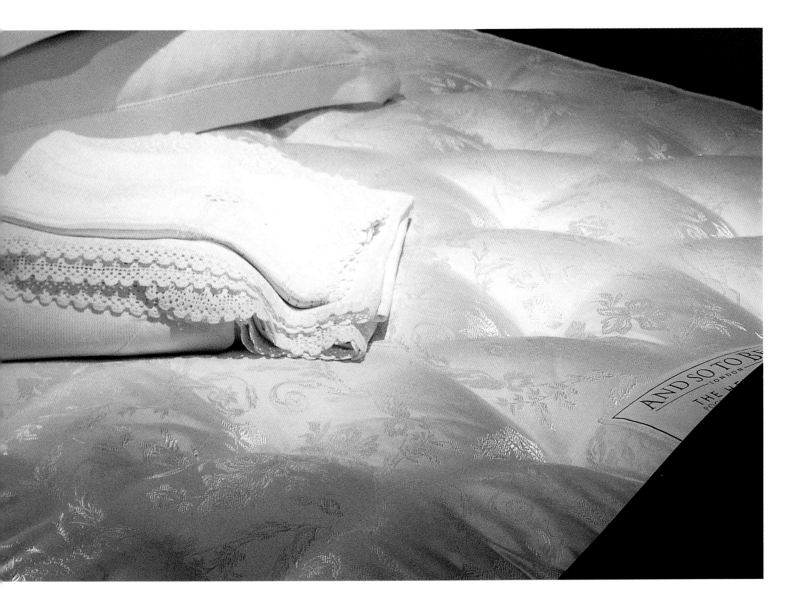

All good bed specialists will display a complete range of mattress sets – from inexpensive open-coil units to top-of-the range two-tier pocket-sprung versions. They will take you through the models displayed on their showroom floor, explain the various options of fillings available and point out the benefits of each upholstery combination. For a couple, they should consider the combined weight of you and your partner and then recommend a suitable model for you to test. Take their advice, lie down on the bed, take your time, and do not be embarrassed. There will be firmer and softer options available, so try these as well. Compare less expensive styles to the more luxurious models and ask what the differences are between them.

English mattress manufacturers make some of the best handmade pocket-sprung beds in the world, but regrettably there are also those who mass produce inexpensive open-coil sets that do little to enhance the tradition of superb quality developed by generations of craftsmen.

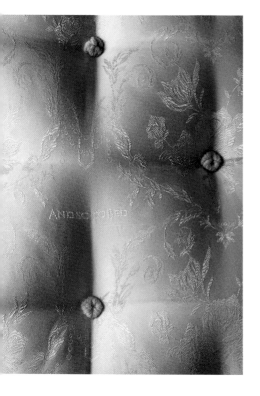

ABOVE *A good-quality mattress should provide comfort and uninterrupted nights for a period of around ten years.*

In basic terms, a mattress consists of three elements: Firstly there is a fabric cover called ticking. This can be made from any type of heavy-duty fabric such as 100 per cent cotton, cotton mixes, rayon or viscose fibres. Unfortunately many cut-price manufacturers use unsuitable, inexpensive lightweight fabrics. The best fabrics are woven jacquards that are manufactured in Belgium. These closely woven fabrics are hair-proofed and flame-resistant.

The second element is the inner core or guts of the mattress, which in most cases is the spring unit. The

ABOVE *Protectors lengthen the life of a mattress and reduce dust mites, which cause skin irritation and allergies in many people.*

RIGHT *Duck and goose down are supremely natural and comfortable, but allergy sufferers need fibre-filled bed coverings.*

spring units can be either an open-coil or pocket-spring type. Springs are made from high-tensile steel. The open-coil model incorporates hourglass-shaped springs that are linked together for stability. This type of spring unit is used in most ordinary beds. Pocket springs are 5cm(2in) diameter springs that are enclosed in individual fabric pockets. Once inside the mattress, the springs are nestled together in a honeycomb formation. This enables each spring to move or be depressed individually and allows the mattress to respond to different body weights and shapes.

With this method of springing, bodies do not roll together. Pocket springs are available as a single-layered mattress where a maximum of 1,800 springs will fit into the queen size, or alternatively as a two-tier unit where a maximum of 2,500 springs can be used.

There are two alternatives to springs: these are latex, which is natural rubber combined with an additive for flame retardancy, and water, which is stored in thick polyester leak-proof tubes. These two versions account for a very small section of the UK market but are very popular in the United States and throughout Europe.

The third element is the upholstery fillings; these are the layers above the spring units, the surface just below the fabric. This is vital to the lift and feel of the mattress. Various natural fillings are used including cotton felt, horsehair, merino wool, mohair and cashmere. Manmade fibres are also used with good effect, and hollofill or white fibre are inexpensive alternatives to natural products that have proved very effective for allergy sufferers. It is the application and combination of these fillings that turn an ordinary mattress into a luxurious one. Less expensive versions may include a layer of cotton felt with a layer of white fibre. A layer of wool is then added for additional luxury. A combination of merino wool and hair gently teased together achieves a beautiful sumptuous top surface. Added luxury would be a generous layer of mohair or cashmere. The balance between top surface and springs is very important. As the top surface becomes softer, so more springs are added to the mattress to ensure that the support system is not compromised.

LEFT *Sheets and pillowcases in plain or patterned pale colours are probably the most popular choice for traditional-style beds.*

RIGHT *Pillows come in all sorts of shapes and sizes. Plump, square continental-style pillows make good decorative additions to a bed, while tiny bolster shapes can create a less formal scene.*

The British Bedding Federation recommends that your bed should be changed every ten years. This is particularly advisable from a hygiene point of view. The average person loses a pint to a pint and a half of moisture per night through perspiration, and the mattress will normally absorb this. This period is obviously a general guideline and is dependent on the quality of bed purchased in the first place. Initially your budget may afford only a less expensive mattress set so you will probably need to change the bed sooner. The sensible method is to buy a mattress that will support you through the ten years without collapsing or sagging. The more luxurious styles are made to last longer and in many instances they will support and perform well for up to twenty years before a replacement is necessary.

An important factor to bear in mind when making a selection is that when you last purchased a bed you (and your partner) were several years younger, you were fitter

Beds are available in the following standard sizes:

Single	3'0" wide x 6'3" long (90 x 190cm).
Double	4'6" wide x 6'3" long (135 x 190cm)
Queen	5'0" wide x 6'6" long (150 x 200cm)
Super Queen	5'6" wide x 6'6" long (168 x 200cm)
King	6'0" wide x 6'6" long (180 x 200cm)
Super King	6'6" wide x 6'6" long (200 x 200cm)
Emperor	7'0" wide x 7'0" long (213 x 213cm)

One of the first steps is to measure your bedroom and decide on the size that will suit your needs. The wider the bed the more sleeping room you will have so your sleep quality will improve. As a general rule, your mattress should be at least 12cm(4¾in) longer than your height. This is especially important if you are purchasing a bedstead that has a foot end higher than the mattress. Conversely, feet hanging over the end of the mattress is uncomfortable. The sizes listed above are standard, but all manufacturers will make a bed longer, at an extra cost.

The queen-sized bed is the most popular double bed size, but, more and more couples are opting for the wider king-sized versions. King-sized beds are available as a one-piece mattress or as two single mattresses zipped together. A one-piece mattress is often preferred because the zip fastenings are not always comfortable to sleep on. However, the benefits of having two single mattresses zipped together can outweigh this disadvantage. Firstly, it is possible to zip two mattresses together that have different degrees of firmness and, secondly, a single mattress is easier to turn.

and probably in better physical condition. You may have gained some weight since your last purchase so the style of bed you found so comfortable then may not meet your requirements for the present or into the next decade or so.

Take advice from the specialists and don't be tempted into buying hastily. Bed selection is very personal. A soft feel for a 22-stone man is like sleeping on the floor to an 8-stone lady. Select the bed you feel comfortable on and trust your own judgement.

index

AND SO TO BED

The following is a list of contact and showroom details for the And So To Bed company:

HEAD OFFICE AND SHOWROOM
Royal Mills
Mill Road, Esher
Surrey KT10 8BL
+44 (0)1372 460 660

SHOWROOMS IN LONDON:
638/640 King's Road
London SW6
+44 (0)20 7731 3593

15 Orchard Street
London W1
+44 (0)20 7935 0225

Freephone: 0808 144 4343
www.andsotobed.co.uk

SHOWROOMS IN THE REST OF THE UNITED KINGDOM:
Nottingham, Nottinghamshire
+44 (0)115 924 3673

Tunbridge Wells, Kent
+44 (0)1892 515 099

Cirencester, Gloucestershire
+44 (0)1285 885 595

Oxford, Oxfordshire
+44 (0)1865 204 202

Rake, Nr Petersfield, Hampshire
+44 (0)1730 894 754

Edinburgh, Scotland
+44 (0)131 652 3700

Glasgow, Scotland
+44 (0)141 353 1355

Belfast, Northern Ireland
+44 (0)28 9032 4154

Acknowledgements

All photographs courtesy of And So To Bed, except the following:

After Noah (e-mail: mailorder@afternoah.com): p117, Mel Yates @ Rapid Eye. *Arcaid*: p72, Richard Bryant/p81, Richard Bryant (Hancock Shaker Village, Pittsfield, Massachusetts, USA)/p84, Richard Bryant (Architect: Gian Franco Brignone)/p94, Richard Bryant (Architect: Gale & Prior)/p110, Jeremy Cockayne/p140, Richard Bryant (Architect:Gian Franco Brignone)/p147, Alan Weintraub (Architect: Micahel Dute)/p151, Simon Kenny/Belle (Architect: Larry Eastwood). *Axiom Photographic Agency*: p10, Dexter Hodges/p124, James Morris/p135 above, James Morris. *elizabethwhiting.com*: p23, Michael Dunne/p27/p50/p73, Julian Nieman/p85. *Ifex plc*: p129. *IPC Syndication*: p99, Simon Whitmore/Ideal Home. *The Interior Archive*: p11, Tim Beddow (Designer: Dodo Cunningham-Reid)/p13, Simon Upton (Designer: Marja Walters/Michael Reeves)/p16, Edina van der Wyck (Designer: Mimmi O'Connell)/p19, Simon McBride (Artist: Douglas Andrews)/p22, Fritz von der Schulenburg (Title: Hylinge/Neoclassicism in the North)/p24, Fritz von der Schulenburg (Title: Rosersberg/Neoclassicism in the North)/p25, Andrew Wood/p29, Henry Wilson (Designer: Ernesto Azzulan)/p33, Wayne Vincent/p35, Andrew Wood (Property: Icon)/p36, Simon Upton (Designer: David Hare)/p41, Fritz von der Schulenburg (Designer: Rupert Cavendish)/p42, Tim Beddow (Designer: Dodo Cunningham-Reid)/p43, Henry Wilson (Designer: Florence Lim)/p46, Henry Wilson (Artist: Harrison)/p48, Tim Beddow (Designer: Emma Fole)/p49, Simon McBride (Designer: Clive Jones)/p52, Bob Smith (Owner: Ricardo)/p55, Simon McBride (Property: Old Chapel)/p67, Fritz von der Schulenburg (Designer: Jasper Conran)/p68–69, Edina van der Wyck (Stylist: Katrin Cargill)/p71, Simon Upton (Designer: Anthony Collett)/p74, Edina van der Wyck (Stylist: Katrin Cargill)/p89, Ken Hayden (Property: Dar Tamsna)/p91, Tim Beddow (Designer: Karen Newman)/p93, Tim Beddow (Owner: Luecks)/p96, Tim Beddow/p113, Fritz von der Schulenburg (Designer: Charles Rennie Mackintosh)/p116, Henry Wilson (Designer: Cynthia Grant)/p121, Herbert Ypma (Architect: Yturbe/Contemporary Mexico)/p122, Andrew Wood (Owner: Mandy Coakley)/p126, Henry Wilson (Architect: Ian Chee)/p131, Henry Wilson (Architect: Ian Chee)/p133, Tim Beddow (Architect: John Pawson)/p134, Henry Wilson (Designer: Brett Muldoon)/p139, Ken Hayden/p143, Inside Stock Image Production (Agency: W Waldron/Inside)/p144, Fritz von der Schulenburg (Country: Lamu)/p148: Fritz von der Schulenburg (Property: Pitchford)/p150: Fritz von der Schulenburg (Designer: Jed Johnson). *Mainstream*: p51, Ray Main/p65, Ray Main/p108, Ray Main (Eltham Palace). *neworld design*: p123, The Morrison, Dublin (Designer: John Rocha/Photo Andrew Bradley). *Orbit Design Company*: p127, 130, 132. *Ianthe Ruthven*: p18, (Designer: Charles Rennie Mackintosh)/p53/p62/p75/p77/p88/p105/p149.